혼공 기초 구문

혼공 기초 구문

허준석·신영환 지음

L1

혼공북스

혼공 기초 구문 Level 1

1판 1쇄 2022년 2월 7일
1판 3쇄 2025년 2월 17일

지은이 허준석 신영환
디자인 박새롬
표지그림 김효지
마케팅 두잉글 사업본부
브랜드 혼공북스
펴낸곳 혼공북스
출판등록 제2021-000288호
주 소 04033 서울특별시 마포구 양화로 113 4층(서교동)
전자메일 team@hongong.co.kr

ISBN 979-11-976810-0-4 13740

머리말

혼공!

눈앞에 맛있는 소고기가 있어요. 너무 배고파서 바로 먹고 싶은데 고기가 너무 커서 한 입에 넣을 수가 없어요. 이럴 때 어떻게 해야 하죠?

맞아요. 작게 잘라서 한 입에 쏘옥 넣어서 먹으면 되지요.

영어 읽기도 마찬가지예요. 긴 영어 글을 한방에 읽고 핵심만 쏙쏙 이해하고 싶잖아요? 하지만 긴 글을 한 호흡에 읽어나가는 것은 쉽지가 않아요. 그렇기 때문에 쌤이 말한 소고기의 원리를 적용해 봅시다. 글을 한 입에 들어갈 수 있을 정도의 작은 단위로 잘라보는 거예요. 그 적당한 크기를 보통 문장이라고 하지요.

이렇게 영어 글을 문장 단위로 잘라서 공부하는 것을 구문공부 또는 구문독해라고 해요. 원서 읽기를 술술술 해내는 친구들에게는 필요가 없을 수도 있지만, 한국에서 자란 많은 친구들에게는 한 번쯤 꼬옥 해볼 것을 권한답니다.

특히 문장을 공부하면서 그 속에서 나오는 단어, 문법을 익히고, 우리말을 보면서 영작까지 해본다면 독해는 물론, 수행평가, 지필고사의 기본기까지 한 번에 쌓을 수 있어요.

우리 친구들! 영어는 절대 어렵지 않아요. 선생님과 함께 딱 20일 동안 교재, 강의를 충실히 보고 나면 자신감이 생길 거예요. 걱정말고 즐겁게, 효율적으로 혼공 해봅시다.
이제 준비되었나요? 그럼 다 같이 **Let's get it!**

대표저자 | 혼공 허준석

〈혼공기초구문 레벨 1〉 미리보기

총 4단계의 완공, 혼공 시스템!

1 혼공기초

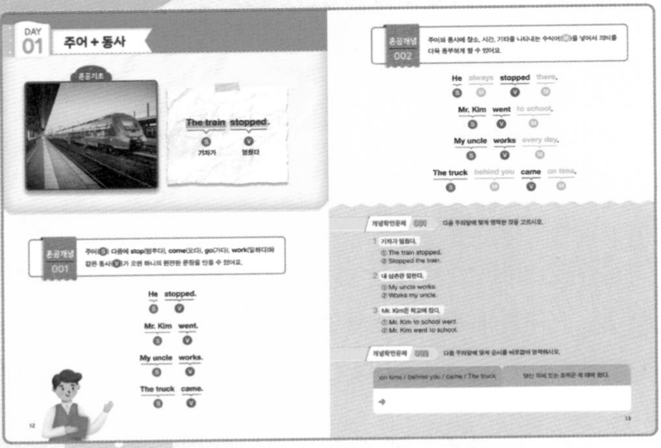

최소의 개념으로 핵심 문장을 공부해요. 적절한 분량의 예문으로 개념을 익히고, 간단한 간접 영작을 통해 적용을 해본답니다. 할 수 있다는 자신감이 생길 거예요.

2 혼공연습

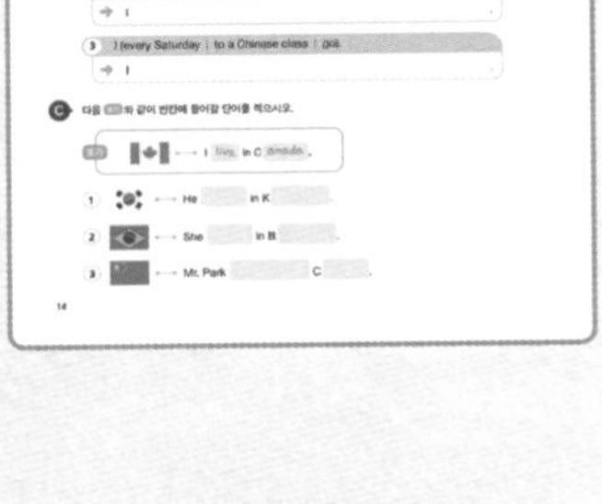

간단한 문항을 풀면서 개념을 반복 적용하고 서서히 확장시켜 나갑니다. 우리말 해석부터 힌트가 주어진 쉬운 영작까지 어렵지 않게 할 수 있어요.

3 혼공완성

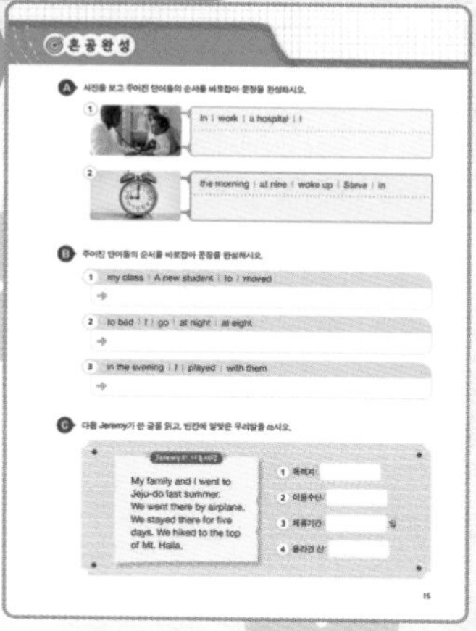

실제 생활과 관련된 사진을 보면서 영작을 한 다음, 힌트가 최소화 된 영작을 하면서 가장 난도가 높은 문제까지 순서대로 다뤄요. 마지막으로, 개념이 적용된 다양한 유형의 문항을 다루면서 실전 감각을 끌어올려요.

4 혼공복습

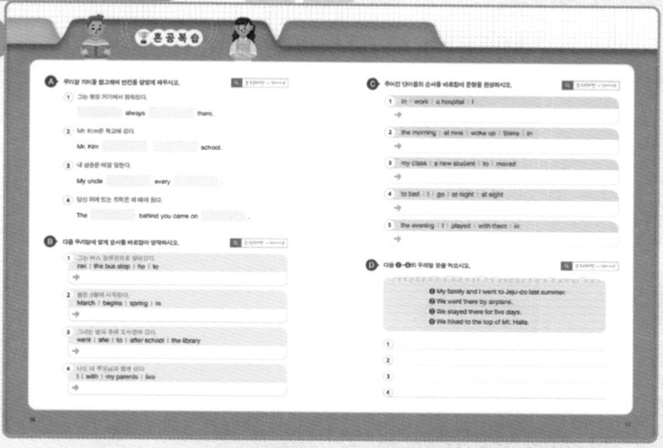

하나의 Day 학습을 효과적으로 마무리 할 수 있는 복습 코너예요. 가장 쉬운 A문항부터, 우리말 의미에 맞게 문장이나 어구를 쓰는 좀 더 어려운 B문항까지 순서대로 제공해요. 이후 더 어려운 C문항의 영작, 마지막 우리말 의미 파악 D문항 까지 체계적으로 풀고 나면 완전학습을 할 수 있어요.

목차

〈혼공기초구문 레벨 1〉

하루 30~40분, 20일만에 기초구문 완전정복하기!

하루 30~40분 집중 학습으로 20일 동안 중학영어 과정에서 알아야 할 기초 구문을 마스터할 수 있는 Study Plan입니다. 학습 후 ◯에 V 표시 하세요.

◯ Day 01	◯ Day 02	◯ Day 03	◯ Day 04	◯ Day 05
주어 + 동사	주어 + 동사 + 보어	주어 + 동사 + 목적어	주어 + 동사 + 목1 + 목2	주어 + 동사 + 목적어 + 목적보어
◯ Day 06	◯ Day 07	◯ Day 08	◯ Day 09	◯ Day 10
현재	과거 / 미래	진행형	현재완료 1	현재완료 2
◯ Day 11	◯ Day 12	◯ Day 13	◯ Day 14	◯ Day 15
조동사 can / could	조동사 may / might	조동사 should / must	기타 조동사	조동사 + have + p.p.
◯ Day 16	◯ Day 17	◯ Day 18	◯ Day 19	◯ Day 20
능동태 / 수동태	수동태의 시제 1	수동태의 시제 2	수동태의 관용표현 1	수동태의 관용표현 2

★ 무료 유튜브 강의와 함께 학습하면 훨씬 더 효율적입니다. 아래의 QR코드를 찍어 보세요!

★ 더 많은 강의는 혼공마켓 클래스룸 (https://hongong.co.kr/classroom)에서 보실 수 있습니다.

N 혼공마켓

Part 1

문장의 뼈대

5형식

- Day 01 The train stopped.
- Day 02 My mother is an artist.
- Day 03 I need ten stamps.
- Day 04 I gave him some money.
- Day 05 Salt makes our food tasty.

DAY 01

주어 + 동사

혼공기초

The train stopped.

S 기차가 V 멈췄다

혼공개념 001

주어(S) 다음에 **stop**(멈추다), **come**(오다), **go**(가다), **work**(일하다)와 같은 동사(V)가 오면 하나의 완전한 문장을 만들 수 있어요.

He (S) **stopped.** (V)

Mr. Kim (S) **went.** (V)

My uncle (S) **works.** (V)

The truck (S) **came.** (V)

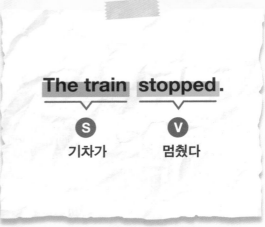

혼공개념 002

주어와 동사에 장소, 시간, 기타를 나타내는 수식어(M)을 넣어서 의미를 더욱 풍부하게 할 수 있어요.

He	always	stopped	there.
S	M	V	M

Mr. Kim	went	to school.
S	V	M

My uncle	works	every day.
S	V	M

The truck	behind you	came	on time.
S	M	V	M

개념확인문제 001

다음 우리말에 맞게 영작한 것을 고르시오.

1 기차가 멈췄다.

① The train stopped.
② Stopped the train.

2 내 삼촌은 일한다.

① My uncle works.
② Works my uncle.

3 Mr. Kim은 학교에 갔다.

① Mr. Kim to school went.
② Mr. Kim went to school.

개념확인문제 002

다음 우리말에 맞게 순서를 바로잡아 영작하시오.

on time / behind you / came / The truck	당신 뒤에 있는 트럭은 제 때에 왔다.
➜	

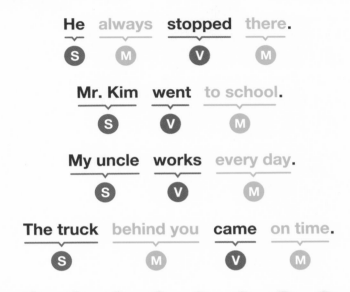

혼공연습

A 다음 문장에서 주어, 동사를 찾아 보기 처럼 S, V라고 쓰시오.

보기
Mike goes to school by bus.
S V

1. He ran to the bus stop.
2. Spring begins in March.
3. She went to the library after school.

B 괄호 안의 단어들을 순서에 맞게 써서 문장을 완성하시오.

1. I (go | at eight | to school).
→ I ______.

2. I (my parents | with | live).
→ I ______.

3. I (every Saturday | to a Chinese class | go).
→ I ______.

C 다음 보기 와 같이 빈칸에 들어갈 단어를 적으시오.

보기

→ I live in Canada.

1.  → He ______ in K______.
2.  → She ______ in B______.
3.  → Mr. Park ______ C______.

혼공완성

A 사진을 보고 주어진 단어들의 순서를 바로잡아 문장을 완성하시오.

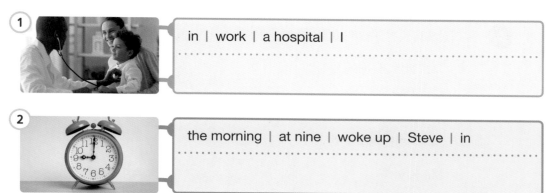

1 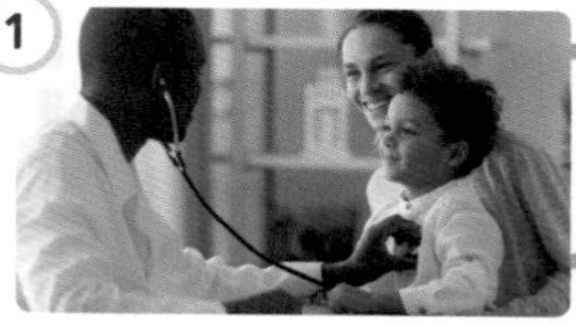

in | work | a hospital | I

2 

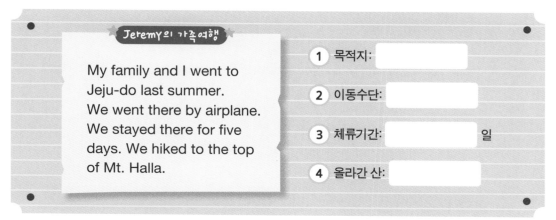

the morning | at nine | woke up | Steve | in

B 주어진 단어들의 순서를 바로잡아 문장을 완성하시오.

1 my class | A new student | to | moved

→

2 to bed | I | go | at night | at eight

→

3 in the evening | I | played | with them

→

C 다음 **Jeremy**가 쓴 글을 읽고, 빈칸에 알맞은 우리말을 쓰시오.

Jeremy의 가족여행

My family and I went to Jeju-do last summer. We went there by airplane. We stayed there for five days. We hiked to the top of Mt. Halla.

1 목적지:

2 이동수단:

3 체류기간: 일

4 올라간 산:

혼공복습

A 우리말 의미를 참고하여 빈칸을 알맞게 채우시오.

잘 모르겠다면 ···› 13페이지로

1 그는 항상 거기에서 멈춰섰다.

_______ always _______ there.

2 Mr. Kim은 학교에 갔다.

Mr. Kim _______ _______ school.

3 내 삼촌은 매일 일한다.

My uncle _______ every _______ .

4 당신 뒤에 있는 트럭은 제 때에 왔다.

The _______ behind you came on _______ .

B 다음 우리말에 맞게 순서를 바로잡아 영작하시오.

잘 모르겠다면 ···› 14페이지로

1 그는 버스 정류장으로 달려갔다.
ran | the bus stop | he | to

→

2 봄은 3월에 시작된다.
March | begins | spring | in

→

3 그녀는 방과 후에 도서관에 갔다.
went | she | to | after school | the library

→

4 나는 내 부모님과 함께 산다.
I | with | my parents | live

→

C 주어진 단어들의 순서를 바로잡아 문장을 완성하시오.

잘 모르겠다면 ···› 15페이지로

1 in | work | a hospital | I

➜

2 the morning | at nine | woke up | Steve | in

➜

3 my class | a new student | to | moved

➜

4 to bed | I | go | at night | at eight

➜

5 the evening | I | played | with them | in

➜

D 다음 ❶~❹의 우리말 뜻을 적으시오.

잘 모르겠다면 ···› 15페이지로

❶ My family and I went to Jeju-do last summer.
❷ We went there by airplane.
❸ We stayed there for five days.
❹ We hiked to the top of Mt. Halla.

1

2

3

4

DAY 02 주어 + 동사 + 보어

혼공기초

My mother is an artist.

S V C

내 어머니는 예술가이다

혼공개념 001

주어(S) 다음에 **be**동사(**am, is, are, was, were**)가 오고 그 다음에 주어를 설명해주는 보어(C)로 형용사나 명사가 와요. '**get** + 형용사'는 이 상태가 된다는 것을 의미해요.

My sister is a high school student.
S V C

He is tall and handsome.
S V C

She is friendly to me.
S V C M

My puppy got sick.
S V C

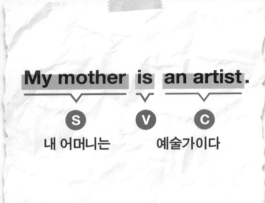

혼공개념 002

be동사 외의 감각동사(**feel**, **look**, **sound**, **taste**)가 온 다음, 상태를 나타내는 형용사가 쓰여서 주어를 설명해주기도 해요.

Your car	looks	good!
S	V	C

This soup	tastes	delicious.
S	V	C

Your idea	sounds	great.
S	V	C

I	often	feel	sleepy and tired.
S	M	V	C

개념확인문제 001 다음 우리말에 맞게 영작한 것을 고르시오.

1 그녀는 나에게 친절하다.

① She is to friendly me.
② She is friendly to me.

2 이 수프는 맛있는 맛이 난다.

① This soup tastes delicious.
② This soup delicious tastes.

3 네 생각은 대단한 것 처럼 들린다.

① Your idea sounds great.
② Sounds your idea great.

개념확인문제 002 다음 우리말에 맞게 순서를 바로잡아 영작하시오.

and / often / feel / I / sleepy / tired	나는 종종 졸리며 피곤하다고 느낀다.

➜

혼공연습

A 다음 문장에서 주어, 동사, 보어를 찾아 보기 처럼 S, V, C라고 쓰시오.

보기

My father is an engineer.
S V C

1. Yesterday was Parents' Day.

2. Your computer looks nice.

3. I am good at Korean.

B 괄호 안의 단어들을 순서에 맞게 써서 문장을 완성하시오.

1. I (not | am | an animal).
→ I ______________________.

2. She (morning | a | is | person).
→ She ______________________.

3. The weather (so | nice | is).
→ The weather ______________________.

C 다음 문장을 우리말로 해석하시오.

1. Forests / are very important / to us.
→

2. Sports / are good / for your health and mind.
→

혼공완성

A 사진을 보고 주어진 단어들의 순서를 바로잡아 문장을 완성하시오.

1

is | Water | important | very

2

is | favorite | My | subject | English

B 주어진 단어들의 순서를 바로잡아 문장을 완성하시오.

1 pet | Coco | my | is | dog

➜

2 Yesterday | sister's | my | was | day | wedding

➜

3 dangerous | rainy | Climbing | days | is | on

➜

C 다음은 반 친구 **Chloe**를 조사한 글이다. 이것을 우리말로 옮겼을 때 잘못된 문장 두 개를 찾아 바르게 고치시오.

- Chloe always looks busy. She's not a night person. Her favorite sports are swimming and tennis. She is healthy and active.
- *클로이는 항상 한가해 보인다. 그녀는 저녁형 인간이 아니다. 그녀가 가장 좋아하는 스포츠는 수영과 테니스 이다. 그녀는 건강하고 활동적이지 않다.*

잘못된 문장	바른 해석
①	
②	

혼공복습

A 우리말 의미를 참고하여 빈칸을 알맞게 채우시오. 잘 모르겠다면 ··· 19페이지로

1. 네 차는 멋져 보여!

   Your ______ ______ good!

2. 이 수프는 맛있는 맛이 난다.

   This ______ ______ delicious.

3. 네 생각은 대단한 것 처럼 들린다.

   Your ______ ______ great.

4. 나는 종종 졸리며 피곤하다고 느낀다.

   I ______ feel sleepy and ______.

B 다음 우리말에 맞게 순서를 바로잡아 영작하시오. 잘 모르겠다면 ··· 20페이지로

1. 어제는 어버이 날이었다.
   Parents' | yesterday | was | Day
   ➜

2. 나는 한국어를 잘한다.
   at Korean | am | I | good
   ➜

3. 나는 동물이 아니다.
   not | I | an animal | am
   ➜

4. 그녀는 아침형 인간이다.
   morning | is | a | she | person
   ➜

C 주어진 단어들의 순서를 바로잡아 문장을 완성하시오.

잘 모르겠다면 ···› 21페이지로

1 is | water | important | very

➜

2 is | favorite | my | subject | English

➜

3 pet | Coco | my | is | dog

➜

4 yesterday | sister's | my | was | day | wedding

➜

5 dangerous | rainy | climbing | days | is | on

➜

D 다음 ❶~❹의 우리말 뜻을 적으시오.

잘 모르겠다면 ···› 21페이지로

❶ Chloe always looks busy.
❷ She's not a night person.
❸ Her favorite sports are swimming and tennis.
❹ She is healthy and active.

1

2

3

4

DAY 03 주어 + 동사 + 목적어

혼공기초

I need ten stamps.
S V O
나는 10장의 우표를 필요로 한다

혼공개념 001

주어(S) 다음에 일반적인 동작을 나타내는 동사(V)가 오고 그 뒤에 목적어(O)가 올 수 있어요. 이 때 목적어(O)는 '~을, 를'로 해석해요.

I broke my leg.
S V O

We saw a beautiful beach.
S V O

Jack took a deep breath.
S V O

Salt has historical meaning.
S V O

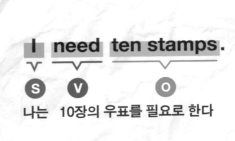

혼공개념 002

목적어(O)는 보어(C)와 달리 주어(S)의 상태를 나타내지 않아요.

He (S) faced (V) strong winds. (O) — He ≠ strong winds

My sister (S) cleaned (V) the living room. (O) — My sister ≠ the living room

In Korea (M) we (S) have (V) four seasons. (O) — We ≠ four seasons

My mom (S) made (V) *bibimbap* (O) for us (M). — My mom ≠ *bibimbap*

개념확인문제 001

다음 우리말에 맞게 영작한 것을 고르시오.

1 나는 10장의 우표가 필요하다.

① I ten stamps need.
② I need ten stamps.

2 Jack은 깊은 숨을 쉬었다.

① Jack took a deep breath.
② Jack a deep took breath.

3 그는 강한 바람을 마주쳤다.

① Faced he strong winds.
② He faced strong winds.

개념확인문제 002

다음 우리말에 맞게 순서를 바로잡아 영작하시오.

made / for us / My mom / *bibimbap*	내 엄마는 우리들을 위해 비빔밥을 만들어 주셨다.

➜

혼공연습

A 다음 문장에서 주어, 동사, 목적어를 찾아 보기 처럼 S, V, O라고 쓰시오.

보기

He	began	climbing	at age 16.
S	V	O	

1 He left his bag at home.

2 She saved money for them.

3 I lost my movie ticket on the subway.

B 괄호 안의 단어들을 순서에 맞게 써서 문장을 완성하시오.

1 We (in | stars | saw | many | the sky).

→ We ______.

2 We (the park | gave | at | a concert).

→ We ______.

3 Minsu (some | watered | plants).

→ Minsu ______.

C 다음 문장을 우리말로 해석하시오.

1 I / usually / start my homework / late at night.

→

2 My puppy / has big ears / and short legs.

→

혼공완성

A 사진을 보고 주어진 단어들의 순서를 바로잡아 문장을 완성하시오.

1 

her bags | started | Nora | packing

2 

with cell phones | We | do | useful | many | things

B 주어진 단어들의 순서를 바로잡아 문장을 완성하시오.

1 mountains | people | like | Many | climbing

→

2 many | The builders | amazing | building techniques | used

→

3 reason | never | missed | He | practice | for | any

→

C 다음 문장 중 'S + V + O의 구조'가 아닌 문장의 번호를 하나 쓰고, 그 문장을 우리말로 해석하시오.

① You can broaden your horizons.
② He hurt his back very badly.
③ Water is very important.
④ The male paints the nest with the juice from blueberries.

번호: ______________

해석: ______________________________________

혼공복습

A 우리말 의미를 참고하여 빈칸을 알맞게 채우시오.

잘 모르겠다면 ⋯ 25페이지로

1 그는 강한 바람을 마주쳤다.

He ______ ______ winds.

2 내 여동생은 거실을 청소했다.

My sister ______ the living ______.

3 한국에는 우리에게 4계절이 있다.

In ______ we have four ______.

4 내 엄마는 우리들을 위해 비빔밥을 만들어 주셨다.

My mom ______ *bibimbap* for ______.

B 다음 우리말에 맞게 순서를 바로잡아 영작하시오.

잘 모르겠다면 ⋯ 26페이지로

1 그는 그의 가방을 집에 두었다.
bag | at | left | he | his | home

➜

2 그녀는 그들을 위해 돈을 절약했다.
saved | she | for | money | them

➜

3 나는 지하철에서 내 영화 티켓을 잃어버렸다.
I | lost | my | on | the subway | movie ticket

➜

4 우리는 하늘에 있는 많은 별들을 보았다.
the sky | stars | saw | many | in | we

➜

C 주어진 단어들의 순서를 바로잡아 문장을 완성하시오.

잘 모르겠다면 ···› 27페이지로

1 at night | usually | my | start | homework | late | I

→

2 packing | bags | Nora | started | her

→

3 do | we | many | things | with | useful | cell phones

→

4 mountains | people | many | like | climbing

→

5 never | he | practice | missed | any | for | reason

→

D 다음 ❶~❹의 우리말 뜻을 적으시오.

잘 모르겠다면 ···› 27페이지로

❶ You can broaden your horizons.
❷ He hurt his back very badly.
❸ Water is very important.
❹ The male paints the nest with the juice from blueberries.

1

2

3

4

주어 + 동사 + 목1 + 목2

혼공기초

I	gave	him	some money.
S	V	O1	O2

나는 　 그에게 약간의 돈을 주었다

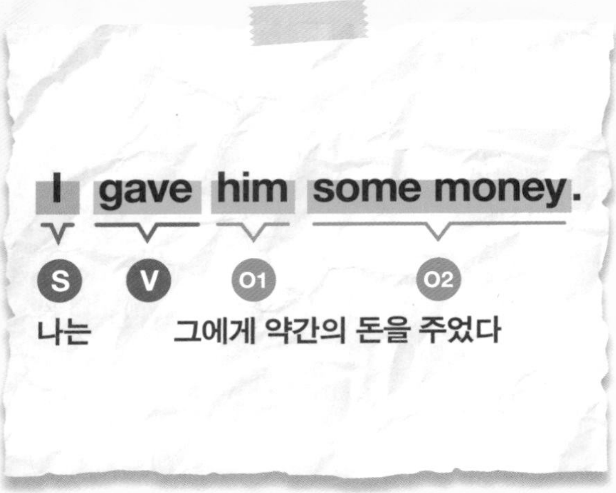

혼공개념 001 ‘준다’라는 의미를 가지고 있는 동사 다음에는 사람(O1), 사물(O2) 두 개의 목적어가 올 수 있어요. 이 때 O1를 간접목적어(I.O.), O2를 직접목적어(D.O.) 라고 한답니다.

Mr. Kim	gave	me	a small job.
S	V	O1	O2

Hermione	told	Harry	everything.
S	V	O1	O2

My uncle	bought	me	a new computer.
S	V	O1	O2

The detective	asked	us	a few questions.
S	V	O1	O2

혼공개념 002

4형식 문장은 비슷한 의미를 가진 3형식 문장으로 바꿀 수 있어요. 이때 문장 마지막에 전치사(**to**, **for**, **of**) + 목적어1(간접목적어)가 온답니다.

Mr. Kim (S) **gave** (V) **a small job** (O) **to me** (M).

Hermione (S) **told** (V) **everything** (O) **to Harry** (M).

My uncle (S) **bought** (V) **a new computer** (O) **for me** (M).

The detective (S) **asked** (V) **a few questions** (O) **of us** (M).

개념확인문제 001 다음 우리말에 맞게 영작한 것을 고르시오.

1 나는 그에게 약간의 돈을 주었다.

① I gave him some money.
② I gave some money him.

2 Hermione는 Harry에게 모든 것을 말했다.

① Hermione told everything Harry.
② Hermione told Harry everything.

3 그 형사는 우리들에게 약간의 질문을 했다.

① The detective asked a few questions to us.
② The detective asked a few questions of us.

개념확인문제 002 다음 우리말에 맞게 순서를 바로잡아 영작하시오.

for me / My uncle / a new computer / bought	내 삼촌은 나를 위해 새 컴퓨터를 사 주셨다.
➜	

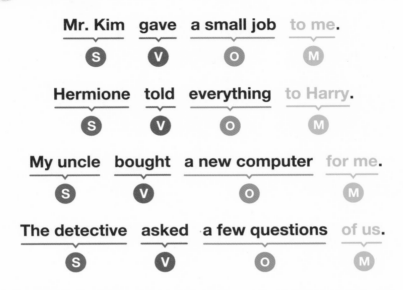

혼공연습

A 다음 문장에서 주어, 동사, 간접목적어, 직접목적어를 찾아 보기 처럼 S, V, O1, O2라고 쓰시오.

보기
He gave you a 50% discount.
S V O1 O2

1. It gives you some exercise.

2. Ms. Kim teaches us Spanish.

3. My mom always makes me delicious food.

B 괄호 안의 단어들을 순서에 맞게 써서 문장을 완성하시오.

1. He (the schedule | me | sent).
➜ He ______________________.

2. My aunt (a video | me | showed).
➜ My aunt ______________________.

3. The woman (us | her | phone | lent).
➜ The woman ______________________.

C 다음 문장을 우리말로 해석하시오.

1. Forests / give / us / fresh air.
➜

2. My father / always / sends / me / text messages / after school.
➜

혼공완성

A 사진을 보고 주어진 단어들의 순서를 바로잡아 문장을 완성하시오.

1

gave | me | Lego castle | the | Jason

2

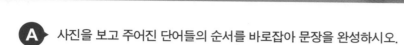

old pictures | showed | me | parents | their | My

B 주어진 단어들의 순서를 바로잡아 문장을 완성하시오.

1 her | gave | The pirates | the secret ring

→

2 where to go | told | him | Malfoy

→

3 about the guy | asked | a lot of | The police officer | questions | me

→

C 다음 문장을 비슷한 의미를 가진 다른 문장으로 바꾸었을 때 빈칸에 들어갈 부분을 완성하시오.

❶ Forests give us fresh air.
= Forests give fresh air ______ .

❷ The reporter asked the movie director a question.
= The reporter asked a question ______ .

1 ______

2 ______

혼공복습

A 우리말 의미를 참고하여 빈칸을 알맞게 채우시오.

잘 모르겠다면 ···› 31페이지로

1. Mr. Kim은 나에게 작은 일을 주었다.

   Mr. Kim ________ me a small ________ .

2. Hermione는 Harry에게 모든 것을 말했다.

   Hermione ________ Harry ________ .

3. 내 삼촌은 나를 위해 새 컴퓨터를 사 주셨다.

   My uncle ________ me a new ________ .

4. 그 형사는 우리들에게 약간의 질문을 했다.

   The detective ________ us a few ________ .

B 다음 우리말에 맞게 순서를 바로잡아 영작하시오.

잘 모르겠다면 ···› 32페이지로

1. Ms. Kim은 우리들에게 스페인어를 가르쳐주신다.
   us | teaches | Ms. Kim | Spanish
   ➜

2. 내 엄마는 항상 나에게 맛있는 음식을 만들어주신다.
   delicious | always | my mom | me | makes | food
   ➜

3. 숲은 우리들에게 신선한 공기를 준다.
   us | fresh | give | forests | air
   ➜

4. 내 아버지는 방과 후에 항상 나에게 문자를 보내주신다.
   always | my father | me | sends | after school | text messages
   ➜

C 주어진 단어들의 순서를 바로잡아 문장을 완성하시오.

잘 모르겠다면 ···› 33페이지로

1 gave | me | Lego castle | the | Jason

→

2 old pictures | showed | me | their | my parents

→

3 her | gave | the pirates | the secret ring

→

4 where to go | told | him | Malfoy

→

5 about the guy | asked | a lot of | the police officer | questions | me

→

D ❶~❸의 문장을 비슷한 의미를 가진 다른 문장으로 바꾸었을 때 빈칸에 들어갈 부분을 완성하시오.

잘 모르겠다면 ···› 33페이지로

❶ Forests give us fresh air.
= Forests give fresh air ________.

❷ The reporter asked the movie director a question.
= The reporter asked a question ________.

❸ My uncle bought me a new computer.
= My uncle bought a new computer ________.

1 ________ 2 ________ 3 ________

DAY 05

주어 + 동사 + 목적어 + 목적보어

혼공기초

Salt makes our food tasty.

S V O O.C.

소금은 만든다 우리의 음식을 맛있게

혼공개념 001

목적어(O) 다음에 형용사나 명사가 와서 목적어에 대해 말해주는 것을 목적보어(O.C.)라고 해요.

My grandfather (S) named (V) the dog (O) Mudge. (O.C.)

They (S) call (V) Chicago (O) the Windy City. (O.C.)

It (S) makes (V) me (O) angry. (O.C.)

The lady (S) found (V) the box (O) empty. (O.C.)

혼공개념 002

목적보어(O.C.)에 동작을 나타내는 표현이 오면 목적어의 행동을 나타낼 수 있어요.

Nora	heard	her mom	shout.
S	V	O	O.C.

She	saw	her neighbor	standing.
S	V	O	O.C.

My parents	want	me	to study.
S	V	O	O.C.

He	also	makes	us	laugh	a lot.
S	M	V	O	O.C.	M

개념확인문제 001

다음 우리말에 맞게 영작한 것을 고르시오.

1 내 할아버지께서 그 개를 Mudge라고 이름지으셨다.

① My grandfather named Mudge the dog.
② My grandfather named the dog Mudge.

2 그것은 나를 화나게 만든다.

① It makes me angry.
② It makes angry me.

3 Nora는 그녀의 엄마가 고함치는 것을 들었다.

① Nora heard her mom shout.
② Nora shouted her mom heard.

개념확인문제 002

다음 우리말에 맞게 순서를 바로잡아 영작하시오.

also / a lot / makes / He / us / laugh	그는 또한 우리들을 많이 웃게 한다.

➜

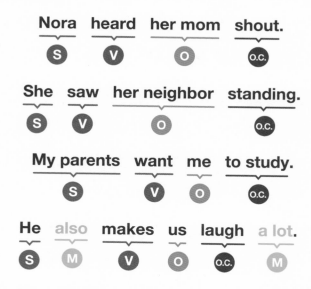

혼공연습

A 다음 문장에서 주어, 동사, 목적어, 목적보어를 찾아 보기 처럼 S, V, O, O.C.라고 쓰시오.

보기
He found it fun.
S V O O.C.

1. It makes your mind calm.

2. Dr. Park advised me to work out regularly.

3. Riding bicycles instead of driving cars can keep it clean.

B 괄호 안의 단어들을 순서에 맞게 써서 문장을 완성하시오.

1. We (keep | clean | rivers).
   ➜ We ________________.

2. David (him | asks | to help) you.
   ➜ David ________________ you.

3. Hogwarts (to fight back | wants | us).
   ➜ Hogwarts ________________.

C 다음 문장을 우리말로 해석하시오.

1. Dirty water / makes / plants and animals / sick.
   ➜

2. Playing sports / can make / your body / strong.
   ➜

혼공완성

A 사진을 보고 주어진 단어들의 순서를 바로잡아 문장을 완성하시오.

1

cry | made | The ending | everyone

2

mistakes | My | them | made | silly | angry

B 주어진 단어들의 순서를 바로잡아 문장을 완성하시오.

1 the school flag | was watching | raise | He | Mrs. Harris

➜

2 elected | president | Lincoln | their | People

➜

3 to the song | He | wanted | me | to listen

➜

C 다음은 인물 보고서의 마지막 부분이다. 보기의 단어를 알맞게 빈칸에 채우시오.

Stella's ________ ________ eventually ________ her ________ a national swimming ____________.

Jun S. Heo

보기 competition / helped / work / win / hard

혼공복습

A 우리말 의미를 참고하여 빈칸을 알맞게 채우시오.

잘 모르겠다면 ... 37페이지로

1 내 할아버지는 그 개를 Mudge라고 이름지었다.

My grandfather ______ the ______ Mudge.

2 그 여인은 그 상자가 빈 것을 발견했다.

The lady ______ the box ______.

3 Nora는 그녀의 엄마가 고함치는 것을 들었다.

Nora ______ her mom ______.

4 그는 또한 우리들을 많이 웃게 한다.

He also ______ us ______ a lot.

B 다음 우리말에 맞게 순서를 바로잡아 영작하시오.

잘 모르겠다면 ... 38페이지로

1 그것은 너의 마음을 차분하게 만든다.
makes | it | mind | your | calm

➜

2 차를 운전하는 것 대신에 자전거를 타는 것은 그것을 깨끗하게 유지시킬 수 있다.
instead of | clean | riding bicycles | driving cars | it | can keep

➜

3 Hogwarts는 우리들이 맞서 싸우기를 원한다.
fight | wants | us | Hogwarts | to | back

➜

4 더러운 물은 식물들과 동물들을 아프게 만든다.
sick | water | dirty | and | makes | animals | plants

➜

C 주어진 단어들의 순서를 바로잡아 문장을 완성하시오.

잘 모르겠다면 ···› 39페이지로

1 can make | your body | strong | playing sports

→

2 cry | made | the ending | everyone

→

3 mistakes | my | them | made | silly | angry

→

4 elected | president | Lincoln | their | people

→

5 to the song | he | wanted | me | to listen

→

D 다음 ❶~❹의 우리말 뜻을 적으시오.

잘 모르겠다면 ···› 39페이지로

❶ Salt makes our food tasty.
❷ She saw her neighbor standing there.
❸ My parents want me to be a scientist.
❹ Stella's hard work eventually helped her win a national swimming competition.

1

2

3

4

Part 2

시간 표현하기

시제

- Day 06 I enjoy playing tennis in my free time.
- Day 07 I finished my homework.
- Day 08 He is reading a book on the bench.
- Day 09 I have known Sam for 10 years.
- Day 10 We have just finished the project.

13
7
20
14
21
15

DAY 06 현재

혼공기초

I / enjoy playing tennis / in my free time.

나는 / 테니스 치는 것을 즐긴다 / 내 여가시간에

혼공개념 001

현재시제는 현재 상황을 나타내지만, 반복되는 일, 습관을 말하기도 해요. 주어가 3인칭 단수일 때는 동사의 마지막에 **s**, **es**를 주로 붙여서 주어와 동사를 잘 구분할 수 있도록 해줘요.

She looks like a rabbit. 현재상황

This cookie tastes delicious. 현재상황

I work in a hospital. 반복되는 일

I often feel sleepy and tired. 반복되는 일

혼공개념 002

현재시제를 써서 일반적인 사실, 진리를 나타낼 수 있어요. 또한 이동(**come, go, leave**)이나 시작과 끝을 나타내는 동사(**start, finish**)의 현재시제로도 '미래'를 표현할 수 있어요.

The museum opens at 10:00 a.m. 일반적인 사실

The sun sets in the west. 일반적인 진리

A good medicine tastes bitter. 일반적인 진리

The train for Seoul leaves soon. 가까운 미래

개념확인문제 001 다음 우리말에 맞게 영작한 것을 고르시오.

1 이 쿠키는 맛이 있다.

① This cookie tastes delicious.
② This cookie tasted delicious.

2 그 박물관은 10시에 연다.

① The museum opens at 10:00 a.m.
② The museum opened at 10:00 a.m.

3 몸에 좋은 약은 쓰다.

① A good medicine tasted bitter.
② A good medicine tastes bitter.

개념확인문제 002 다음 우리말에 맞게 순서를 바로잡아 영작하시오.

sets / in / The sun / the west	해는 서쪽에서 진다.
→	

혼공연습

A 다음 문장에서 밑줄 친 현재시제가 표현하는 의미를 '현재상황', '반복되는 일', '일반적인 진리', '가까운 미래' 중 하나 골라서 쓰시오.

보기
I / work in a hospital.
반복되는 일

1 The midterms / start in a week.

____

2 My friends / always copy my homework.

____

3 His speech / sounds great.

____

B 괄호 안의 단어들을 순서에 맞게 써서 문장을 완성하시오.

1 I (to music | like | listening).
➜ I ______________________.

2 We (school food | like | our).
➜ We ______________________.

3 I (baseball | with | play | after school | the team).
➜ I ______________________.

C 다음 문장을 우리말로 해석하시오.

1 Sports are important / for our health.
➜

2 The post office closes / at half past five.
➜

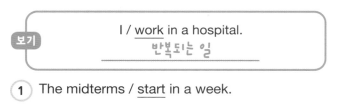

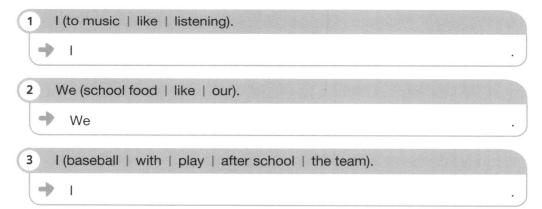

혼공완성

A 사진을 보고 주어진 단어들의 순서를 바로잡아 문장을 완성하시오.

1
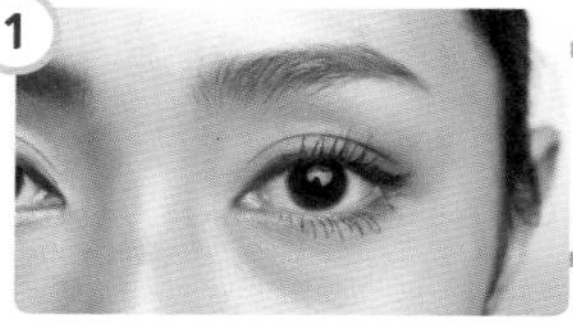

eyes | has | She | beautiful

2

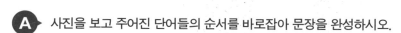

cell phones | make | We | movies | with

B 주어진 단어들의 순서를 바로잡아 문장을 완성하시오.

1 brings | Tourism | into | a country | money

➜

2 gives | you | for | Breakfast | energy | the day

➜

3 have | Rivers | benefits | many

➜

C 다음은 내가 나에 대해 작성한 글이다. 우리말로 요약한 내용의 빈칸에 알맞은 단어를 쓰시오.

I'm fourteen years old. I like playing soccer on the playground. I usually start my homework late at night. I have difficulty speaking in front of people.

나이: ________ 살　　좋아하는 운동: ________

숙제하는 시간: ________ 밤

어려워하는 점: ________________

혼공복습

A 우리말 의미를 참고하여 빈칸을 알맞게 채우시오.

잘 모르겠다면 ···› 44페이지로

1 나는 내 여가시간에 테니스 치는 것을 즐긴다.

I ______ playing tennis in my ______ time.

2 그녀는 토끼같이 보인다.

She ______ like a ______ .

3 그 박물관은 10시에 연다.

The ______ ______ at 10:00 a.m.

4 몸에 좋은 약은 쓰다.

A good ______ tastes ______ .

B 다음 우리말에 맞게 순서를 바로잡아 영작하시오.

잘 모르겠다면 ···› 46페이지로

1 해는 서쪽에서 진다.
in | sets | the sun | the west

➜

2 내 친구들은 항상 내 숙제를 베낀다.
always | friends | my | homework | copy | my

➜

3 나는 방과 후에 그 팀과 야구를 한다.
baseball | with | play | I | after school | the team

➜

4 스포츠는 당신의 건강을 위해 중요하다.
are | sports | your | important | health | for

➜

C 주어진 단어들의 순서를 바로잡아 문장을 완성하시오.

잘 모르겠다면 ···› 47페이지로

1. eyes | has | she | beautiful

→

2. cell phones | make | we | movies | with

→

3. brings | tourism | into | a country | money

→

4. gives | you | for | breakfast | energy | the day

→

5. have | rivers | benefits | many

→

D 다음 ❶~❹의 우리말 뜻을 적으시오.

잘 모르겠다면 ···› 47페이지로

❶ I'm fourteen years old.
❷ I like playing soccer on the playground.
❸ I usually start my homework late at night.
❹ I have difficulty speaking in front of people.

1

2

3

4

과거 / 미래

혼공기초

I / finished my homework.

나는 / 내 숙제를 끝마쳤다

혼공개념 001

이미 지나간 상태나 동작을 말할 때 과거시제를 사용해요. 지나간 일이고 현재는 어떠한 상황인지 알 수 없답니다.

He built a successful computer company.

Jiho won the singing contest.

Sam and Jenny had fun today.

They set up a tent and cooked together.

혼공개념 002

'**will** + 동사원형', '**be going to** + 동사원형'을 쓰면 미래시제를 나타낼 수 있어요.

We will meet at nine in front of the school.

I will go on a picnic with my friends this Saturday.

I am going to watch a movie with my family in the evening.

I am going to tell you about my mom.

개념확인문제 001 다음 우리말에 맞게 영작한 것을 고르시오.

1 나는 내 숙제를 끝마쳤다.

① I finish my homework.
② I finished my homework.

2 Jiho는 노래 대회에서 우승했다.

① Jiho wins the singing contest.
② Jiho won the singing contest.

3 우리는 학교 앞에서 9시에 만날 것이다.

① We met at nine in front of the school.
② We will meet at nine in front of the school.

개념확인문제 002 다음 우리말에 맞게 순서를 바로잡아 영작하시오.

my mom / I / am going to / you / tell / about	나는 내 엄마에 대해 너에게 말할 것이다.

➜

혼공연습

A 다음 괄호 안의 지시에 맞는 것을 고르시오.

보기 I [buy / bought / will buy] a shirt for my dad at your shop. (과거)

1. Dr. Smith [becomes / became / will become] a doctor in 1930. (과거)
2. I [stay / stayed / will stay] there for a week. (미래)
3. They [spend / spent / will spend] all day swimming at the beach. (미래)

B 괄호 안의 단어들을 순서에 맞게 써서 문장을 완성하시오.

1. I (my | lost | on | movie ticket | the subway).
   → I .
2. I (going | am | to | there | by bus | travel).
   → I .
3. He (writing | at the age of | started | thirteen | computer programs).
   → He .

C 다음 문장을 우리말로 해석하시오.

1. My computer / didn't work last night.
   →
2. We / are also going to make a video.
   →

혼공완성

A 사진을 보고 주어진 단어들의 순서를 바로잡아 문장을 완성하시오.

1

yesterday | I | my | broke | leg

2

will | I | play | for | it | someday | you

B 주어진 단어들의 순서를 바로잡아 문장을 완성하시오.

1 his | put | He | on | clothes

➜

2 umbrella | I | bring | didn't | my

➜

3 Korean history | read | John | about | a book

➜

C 다음은 John의 여름방학 이야기이다. 의미상 (A)~(C)중 잘못된 것을 하나 적고 알맞게 고치시오.

My Trip to Jeonju

I went to Jeonju with my family this summer. We (A) went there by KTX. We (B) visited Hanok Village and had *bibimbap* there. We (C) were going to visit Jeonju next summer.

잘못된 것 ______________ 바른 단어 ______________

혼공복습

A 우리말 의미를 참고하여 빈칸을 알맞게 채우시오.

잘 모르겠다면 ···› 51페이지로

1. 나는 내 숙제를 끝마쳤다.

   I ________ my ________ .

2. Jiho는 노래 대회에서 우승했다.

   Jiho ________ the singing ________ .

3. 우리는 학교 앞에서 9시에 만날 것이다.

   We ________ meet at nine in ________ of the school.

4. 나는 내 엄마에 대해 너에게 말할 것이다.

   I am ________ to ________ you about my mom.

B 다음 우리말에 맞게 순서를 바로잡아 영작하시오.

잘 모르겠다면 ···› 52페이지로

1. Smith 박사는 1930년에 의사가 되었다.
   in | became | a doctor | 1930 | Dr. Smith

   ➜

2. 그들은 해변에서 하루종일 수영하면서 보낼 것이다.
   spend | the beach | they | will | all day | swimming | at

   ➜

3. 나는 거기에 버스로 여행갈 것이다.
   going | am | to | there | by bus | travel | I

   ➜

4. 그는 13세의 나이에 컴퓨터 프로그램 만들기를 시작했다.
   writing | at the age of | he | started | thirteen | computer programs

   ➜

C 주어진 단어들의 순서를 바로잡아 문장을 완성하시오.

잘 모르겠다면 ···› 53페이지로

1 my | didn't | work | computer | night | last

→

2 yesterday | I | my | broke | leg

→

3 his | put | he | on | clothes

→

4 umbrella | I | bring | didn't | my

→

5 Korean history | read | John | about | a book

→

D 다음 ❶~❹의 우리말 뜻을 적으시오.

잘 모르겠다면 ···› 53페이지로

❶ I went to Jeonju with my family this summer.
❷ We went there by KTX.
❸ We visited Hanok Village and had *bibimbap* there.
❹ We are going to visit Jeonju next summer.

1

2

3

4

DAY 08

진행형

혼공기초

He / is reading a book / on the bench.

그는 / 책을 읽는 중이다 / 벤치에서

혼공개념 001

지금 일시적으로 어떤 동작을 하고 있거나 상태를 말할 때 '~하는 중이다' 라는 현재진행형을 써요. **'am / is / are + v-ing'**로 나타낸답니다. 가까운 미래를 표현하는 상황에서는 이미 결정하고 준비된 일을 '~할 것이다'라고 쓰기도 해요.

I'm looking for my dog.

Jane is talking on the phone.

The train is arriving at Seoul Station.

My grandparents are visiting my house tonight. 가까운 미래

혼공개념 002

'was / were + v-ing'로 '~하는 중이었다'는 의미의 과거진행형을 나타낼 수 있어요. 미래형태는 **'will + be + v-ing'**로 '~하는 중일 것이다' 라는 의미를 나타내요.

I was looking for my dog.

Jane was talking on the phone.

The train was arriving at Seoul Station.

They will be waiting for you at the airport.

개념확인문제 001 다음 우리말에 맞게 영작한 것을 고르시오.

1 그는 벤치에서 책을 읽는 중이다.

① He is reading a book on the bench.
② He was reading a book on the bench.

2 Jane은 전화기로 이야기하는 중이다.

① Jane was talking on the phone.
② Jane is talking on the phone.

3 그 기차는 서울역에 도착하는 중이었다.

① The train is arriving at Seoul Station.
② The train was arriving at Seoul Station.

개념확인문제 002 다음 우리말에 맞게 순서를 바로잡아 영작하시오.

waiting / will / They / be / at the airport / for you	그들은 공항에서 너를 기다리는 중일 것이다.

➜

혼공연습

A 다음 문장의 밑줄 친 부분을 바꿔써서 진행형을 완성하시오.

보기 Jenny walks in the park with her dog. (현재진행형)
is walking

1 My sister wears a white dress. (현재진행형)

____

2 He moves a desk. (과거진행형)

____

3 He plays the drums in the choir room. (미래진행형)

____

B 괄호 안의 단어들을 순서에 맞게 써서 문장을 완성하시오.

1 He (washing | the driveway | was | a car | in).

➜ He ______________________.

2 You (being | nice | are | so).

➜ You ______________________.

3 The kids (crossing | not | the road | were).

➜ The kids ______________________.

C 다음 문장을 우리말로 해석하시오.

1 We / are planning / to create a town homepage.

➜

2 The earth / is dying / because of trash.

➜

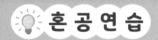

혼공완성

A 사진을 보고 주어진 단어들의 순서를 바로잡아 문장을 완성하시오.

1 

at school | were | They | around | walking

2 

on Hong Kong | I | a TV program | watching | was

B 주어진 단어들의 순서를 바로잡아 문장을 완성하시오.

1 is | class president | running | for | David

→

2 are | day | They | a | having | bad

→

3 was | She | her | disappointment | expressing

→

C 다음은 John이 작성한 환경보고서의 일부이다. 주어진 우리말과 영단어를 참고하여 빈칸에 들어갈 표현을 작성하시오.

- The islands (A) (sink) into the sea. (가라앉고 있는 중이다)
- Jaguars (B) (disappear) in the wild. (사라지고 있는 중이다)

(A) ______________________

(B) ______________________

혼공복습

A 우리말 의미를 참고하여 빈칸을 알맞게 채우시오.

잘 모르겠다면 ···→ 57페이지로

1. 그는 벤치에서 책을 읽는 중이다.

   He is ________ a book on the ________ .

2. Jane은 전화기로 이야기하는 중이다.

   Jane is ________ on the ________ .

3. 그 기차는 서울역에 도착하는 중이었다.

   The train ________ ________ at Seoul Station.

4. 그들은 공항에서 너를 기다리는 중일 것이다.

   They ________ be ________ for you at the airport.

B 다음 우리말에 맞게 순서를 바로잡아 영작하시오.

잘 모르겠다면 ···→ 58페이지로

1. 내 여동생은 하얀색 드레스를 입고 있다.
   sister | my | wearing | is | a white dress

   ➜

2. 그는 합창단실에서 드럼을 연주하는 중일 것이다.
   will | the choir room | he | be | in | the drums | playing

   ➜

3. 그 아이들은 길을 건너고 있는 중이 아니었다.
   crossing | not | the kids | the road | were

   ➜

4. 우리는 마을 홈페이지를 만들려고 계획하고 있는 중이다.
   are | a town homepage | we | planning | to create

   ➜

C 주어진 단어들의 순서를 바로잡아 문장을 완성하시오.

잘 모르겠다면 ···› 59페이지로

1 trash | is | the earth | dying | because of

➜

2 on Hong Kong | I | a TV program | watching | was

➜

3 is | class president | running | for | David

➜

4 are | day | they | a | having | bad

➜

5 was | she | her | disappointment | expressing

➜

D 다음 ❶~❹의 우리말 뜻을 적으시오.

잘 모르겠다면 ···› 59페이지로

❶ Jenny is walking in the park with her dog.
❷ He is moving a desk.
❸ The islands are sinking into the sea.
❹ Jaguars are disappearing in the wild.

1

2

3

4

DAY 09

현재완료 1

혼공기초

I / have known Sam / for 10 years.

나는 / Sam을 알아왔다 / 10년 동안

혼공개념 001

과거의 일이 현재에 영향을 미칠 때 말하는 표현을 '현재완료'라고 해요. 'have(has) + p.p.(과거분사)'로 쓰고 p.p.는 동작에 대한 정보를 전달한답니다.

Mike has written a book.

We have lived in Korea.

My mom has kept the door open.

Mr. Park has taught math in the US.

혼공개념 002

현재완료에는 **'for** + 기간(~동안)', **'since** + 시점(~부터)', **'how long** (얼마나 오랫동안)' 등과 같은 시간표현이 쓰여 과거에 시작한 행동이 현재까지 계속되고 있다는 것을 알려줘요.

Mike has written a book since last year.

We have lived in Korea for 10 years.

My mom has kept the back door open all day.

How long have you taught math?

개념확인문제 001 다음 우리말에 맞게 영작한 것을 고르시오.

1 나는 10년 동안 Sam을 알아왔다.

① I know Sam for 10 years.
② I have known Sam for 10 years.

2 Mike는 작년부터 책을 써왔다.

① Mike has written a book since last year.
② Mike have written a book since last year.

3 우리는 한국에 10년 동안 살아왔다.

① We have lived in Korea for 10 years.
② We have lived in Korea since 10 years.

개념확인문제 002 다음 우리말에 맞게 순서를 바로잡아 영작하시오.

taught / math / How / have / long / you	당신은 얼마나 오랫동안 수학을 가르쳤나요?

➔

혼공연습

A 다음 문장의 밑줄 친 부분을 현재완료 형태로 바꾸시오.

보기 I live in London. (현재완료)
have lived

1 She write a book.

____

2 We know each other.

____

3 My dad keep the door closed.

____

B 괄호 안의 단어들을 순서에 맞게 써서 문장을 완성하시오.

1 Tom (lived | for two months | has | in New York).

➜ Tom _______________.

2 She (waited | has | three hours | for | for | her little sister).

➜ She _______________.

3 We (a long time | have | gathered | for | information).

➜ We _______________.

C 다음 문장을 우리말로 해석하시오.

1 Since then, / Erik / has climbed other very tall mountains.

➜

2 It has been almost a year / since my students and I visited your school.

➜

혼공완성

A 사진을 보고 주어진 단어들의 순서를 바로잡아 문장을 완성하시오.

1 

have | natural wonders | "Good luck" coins | ruined

2 

been | to me | have | for a long time | They | good

B 주어진 단어들의 순서를 바로잡아 문장을 완성하시오.

1 for three months | My dad | exercised | regularly | has

→

2 between them | have | serious | There | arguments | been

→

3 lived | in | He | has | Busan | never

→

C 다음은 산악 등반에 대한 보고서의 마지막 부분이다. 주어진 단어를 의미에 알맞게 변형해서 빈칸을 채우시오. (필요할 경우 단어를 추가할 수 있음)

Mr. Everest

So far, about 5,000 people ______ in climbing to the top of Mt. Everest. (succeed)

혼공복습

A 우리말 의미를 참고하여 빈칸을 알맞게 채우시오.

잘 모르겠다면 ···› 63페이지로

1. 나는 10년 동안 Sam을 알아왔다.

   I have ________ Sam for 10 ________ .

2. Mike는 작년부터 책을 써왔다.

   Mike ________ written a book ________ last year.

3. 우리는 한국에 10년 동안 살아왔다.

   We ________ ________ in Korea for 10 years.

4. 당신은 얼마나 오랫동안 수학을 가르쳤나요?

   How ________ have you ________ math?

B 다음 우리말에 맞게 순서를 바로잡아 영작하시오.

잘 모르겠다면 ···› 64페이지로

1. 내 엄마는 뒷 문을 하루 종일 열어두었다.
   mom | has | my | the back door | kept | all day | open

   ➜

2. Tom은 New York에서 두 달 동안 살고 있다.
   lived | Tom | for two months | has | in New York

   ➜

3. 그녀는 그녀의 여동생을 세 시간 동안 기다렸다.
   waited | has | three hours | for | she | for | her little sister

   ➜

4. 우리는 오랫동안 정보를 모아왔다.
   a long time | have | gathered | we | for | information

   ➜

C 주어진 단어들의 순서를 바로잡아 문장을 완성하시오.

잘 모르겠다면 ···› 65페이지로

1 Erik | climbed | since then | other | very tall | has | mountains

➜

2 have | natural wonders | "good luck" coins | ruined

➜

3 been | to me | have | for a long time | they | good

➜

4 for three months | my dad | exercised | regularly | has

➜

5 between them | have | serious | there | arguments | been

➜

D 다음 ❶~❸의 우리말 뜻을 적으시오.

잘 모르겠다면 ···› 65페이지로

❶ It has been almost a year since my students and I visited your school.
❷ He has never lived in Busan.
❸ So far, about 5,000 people have succeeded in climbing to the top of Mt. Everest.

1

2

3

4

DAY 10

현재완료 2

혼공기초

We / have just finished the project.

우리는 / 막 그 프로젝트를 끝냈다

혼공개념 001

방금 어떤 것을 끝내거나 미처 끝내지 못했을 때 현재완료를 써요. **just**, **already**, **yet**, **now** 등과 함께 쓰인답니다. 현재완료를 써서 과거로 인해 현재 어떤 결과가 나왔는지를 표현할 수도 있어요.

I have already done my homework.

The superheroes have completed the mission now.

I haven't received a text message from her yet.

I have lost my wallet.

혼공개념 002

과거부터 지금까지 '~한 적이 있다'는 경험을 나타낼 때에도 현재완료를 쓴답니다. 주로 **ever**, **never**, **before**, 횟수(**once**, **twice**, **~ times**)와 함께 쓰여요.

James has met my parents before.

My Spanish teacher has never been to Spain.

I have heard music coming from your apartment a few times.

Have you ever driven an electric car before?

개념확인문제 001 다음 우리말에 맞게 영작한 것을 고르시오.

1 우리는 막 그 프로젝트를 끝냈다.

① We haven't finished the project yet.
② We have just finished the project.

2 나는 이미 내 숙제를 다 했다.

① I already done have my homework.
② I have already done my homework.

3 James는 전에 내 부모님과 만난 적이 있다.

① James has met my parents before.
② James met has my parents before.

개념확인문제 002 다음 우리말에 맞게 순서를 바로잡아 영작하시오.

never / to Spain / has / My Spanish teacher / been	내 스페인어 선생님은 절대 스페인에 가본 적이 없다.
→	

혼공연습

A 다음 문장의 빈칸에 들어갈 단어를 보기 에서 골라 한 번씩 쓰시오.

보기 ever already yet

1 Your effort hasn't paid off ____________.

2 Have you ____________ had thoughts like these?

3 They have ____________ gone to bed.

B 괄호 안의 단어들을 순서에 맞게 써서 문장을 완성하시오.

1 I (a foreign country | to | never | have | been).

→ I ____________.

2 She (to | twice | been | has | Jeju-do).

→ She ____________.

3 BTS (a new | just | has | album | released).

→ BTS ____________.

C 다음 문장을 우리말로 해석하시오.

1 We / have met James / three times.

→

2 I / have lost my diary.

→

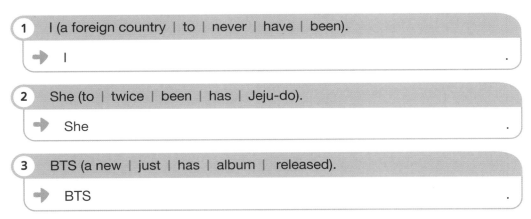

혼공완성

A 사진을 보고 주어진 단어들의 순서를 바로잡아 문장을 완성하시오.

1

the singer | before | have | I | seen

2

lunch | have | We | had | already

B 주어진 것의 순서를 바로잡아 문장을 완성하시오.

1 have | here | I | already | arrived

➜

2 Indian food | before | We | never | tried | have

➜

3 this movie | you | Have | seen | ever | ?

➜

C 다음은 '가장 최근에 한 여행'이라는 주제로 반 친구들을 조사한 결과이다. 표 내용을 참고하여 빈칸에 적절한 영어 단어를 쓰시오.

★ 친구들의 국내 여행 경험 횟수 ★

이름	국내	해외
Jihoo	제주도 3회	필리핀 1회
Haeun	제주도 1회	미국 3회
Sumin	경주 3회	베트남 2회

1 ____________ has been to Jeju-do ____________ times.

2 ____________ has been to Gyeongju ____________ ____________.

혼공복습

A 우리말 의미를 참고하여 빈칸을 알맞게 채우시오.

잘 모르겠다면 → 69페이지로

1. 우리는 막 그 프로젝트를 끝냈다.

   We have ______ ______ the project.

2. 나는 이미 내 숙제를 다 했다.

   I ______ ______ done my homework.

3. James는 전에 내 부모님과 만난 적이 있다.

   James ______ met my parents ______.

4. 내 스페인어 선생님은 절대 스페인에 가본 적이 없었다.

   My Spanish teacher has ______ ______ to Spain.

B 다음 우리말에 맞게 순서를 바로잡아 영작하시오.

잘 모르겠다면 → 70페이지로

1. 너의 노력은 아직 결실을 맺지 못했다.

   yet | effort | hasn't | your | paid off

   →

2. 그들은 이미 잠자러 가버렸다.

   to bed | have | they | already | gone

   →

3. 나는 절대 외국에 가본 적이 없다.

   a foreign country | to | never | have | I | been

   →

4. 그녀는 제주도에 두 번 가본 적이 있다.

   to | twice | she | been | has | Jeju-do

   →

C 주어진 단어들의 순서를 바로잡아 문장을 완성하시오.

잘 모르겠다면 ⋯ 71페이지로

1 a new | just | has | album | released | BTS

➜

2 three times | have | James | met | we

➜

3 the singer | before | have | I | seen

➜

4 lunch | have | We | had | already

➜

5 have | here | I | already | arrived

➜

D 다음 ❶~❹의 우리말 뜻을 적으시오.

잘 모르겠다면 ⋯ 71페이지로

❶ We have never tried Indian food before.
❷ Have you ever seen this movie?
❸ Jihoo has been Jeju-do three times.
❹ Sumin has been to Gyeongju twice.

1

2

3

4

Part 3

정도 표현하기
조동사

- Day 11 We can do many useful things with cell phones.
- Day 12 This may not be easy.
- Day 13 We should take care of them.
- Day 14 People used to pay in gold.
- Day 15 I should have arrived earlier.

Weather News

DAY 11

조동사 can / could

혼공기초

We / can do many useful things / with cell phones.

우리는 / 많은 유용한 것을 할 수 있다 / 휴대폰으로

혼공개념 001

동사 앞에 조동사를 써서 표현의 정도를 나타낼 수 있어요.
can은 '~할 수 있다, ~해도 된다'라는 의미로 능력, 허가를 나타내요.
보통 **can**은 **be able to**로 바꿔 쓸 수 있어요.

I can(am able to) carry people to other places. 능력

Elephants can(are able to) get a message from far away. 능력

We can(are able to) reduce trash in our daily lives. 능력

Can I go to his birthday party? 허가

혼공개념 002

could는 **can**의 과거형이고, '~할 수 있었다'라는 의미로 쓰여요. **was / were able to**로 대신 나타낼 수 있답니다. 또한 현재형보다 한 걸음 물러선 상태이기 때문에 부탁할 때 좀 더 공손한 느낌을 줘요. 마지막으로, 상황에 따라 '~일 수도 있다'라는 추측을 나타낼 수 있어요.

I couldn't(wasn't able to) see the movie. 가능

I couldn't(wasn't able to) finish my homework. 가능

Could you drive me home? 공손한 부탁

It could rain tomorrow. 추측

개념확인문제 001 다음 우리말에 맞게 영작한 것을 고르시오.

1 우리는 휴대폰으로 많은 유용한 것을 할 수 있다.

① We can do many useful things with cell phones.
② We do can many useful things with cell phones.

2 코끼리는 멀리서도 메시지를 전달받을 수 있다.

① Elephants are able to get a message from far away.
② Elephants were able to get a message from far away.

3 내일 비가 올 수도 있어.

① It rain could tomorrow.
② It could rain tomorrow.

개념확인문제 002 다음 우리말에 맞게 순서를 바로잡아 영작하시오.

homework / I / finish / couldn't / my	나는 내 숙제를 끝낼 수 없었다.
➜	

혼공연습

A 다음 문장의 밑줄 친 부분을 보기 처럼 다시 쓰시오.

보기 I make a paper bird.
can make ______________

1 I understand Korean well.

____

2 You have fun playing in the mud.

____

3 You are healthy and happy.

____

B 괄호 안의 단어들을 순서에 맞게 써서 문장을 완성하시오.

1 We (these | can | for | carry | boxes | the old lady).

→ We ______________ .

2 He (a job | not | find | could).

→ He ______________ .

3 I (your project | can | a big help | be | to).

→ I ______________ .

C 다음 문장을 우리말로 해석하시오.

1 Sometimes / climbing / can be dangerous.

→

2 You / can use the new computers / at any time / during school hours.

→

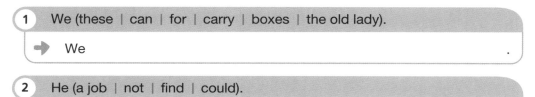

혼공완성

A 사진을 보고 주어진 것의 순서를 바로잡아 문장을 완성하시오.

1

credit card | I | by | pay | Could | ?

2
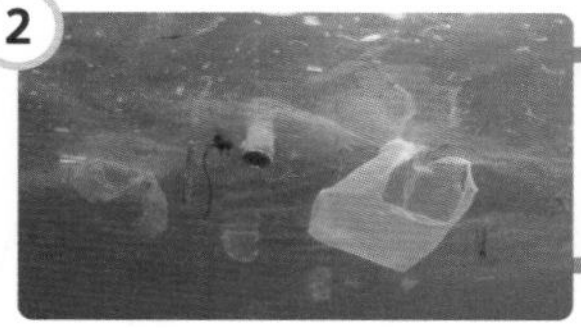

areas | damage | natural | can | Tourism

B 주어진 단어들의 순서를 바로잡아 문장을 완성하시오.

1 can | We | with | clothes | *hanji* | make

→

2 can | public places | cause | Cell phones | problems | in

→

3 her height | the ride | could | get on | not | because of | She

→

C 다음 표지판을 참고하여 빈칸을 적절하게 채우시오.

A: You ______ ______ pictures in this art museum.

B: Oh, I see. Then, can I eat this burger here?

A: No, you ______ eat or ______ anything inside.

혼공복습

A 우리말 의미를 참고하여 빈칸을 알맞게 채우시오.

잘 모르겠다면 ⋯→ 77페이지로

1 우리는 휴대폰으로 많은 유용한 것을 할 수 있다.

We ______ do many ______ things with cell phones.

2 코끼리는 멀리서도 메시지를 전달받을 수 있다.

Elephants are ______ to get a ______ from far away.

3 내일 비가 올 수도 있어.

It ______ ______ tomorrow.

4 나는 내 숙제를 끝낼 수 없었다.

I couldn't ______ my ______ .

B 다음 우리말에 맞게 순서를 바로잡아 영작하시오.

잘 모르겠다면 ⋯→ 78페이지로

1 당신은 진흙 속에서 놀면서 즐거운 시간을 보낼 수 있다.
you | in the mud | have | can | fun | playing

→

2 당신은 건강하고 행복해질 수 있다.
can | healthy | be | you | happy | and

→

3 나는 당신의 프로젝트에 큰 도움이 될 수 있다.
your project | can | a big help | be | to | I

→

4 때때로 등산은 위험할 수 있다.
dangerous | climbing | can | sometimes | be

→

C 주어진 것의 순서를 바로잡아 문장을 완성하시오.

잘 모르겠다면 ..., 79페이지로

1 credit card | I | by | pay | could | ?

➜

2 areas | damage | natural | can | tourism

➜

3 can | we | with | clothes | *hanji* | make

➜

4 can | public places | cause | cell phones | problems | in

➜

5 her height | the ride | could | get on | not | because of | she

➜

D 다음 ❶~❹의 우리말 뜻을 적으시오.

잘 모르겠다면 ..., 79페이지로

❶ You can't take pictures in this art museum.
❷ Oh, I see.
❸ Then, can I eat this burger here?
❹ No, you can't eat or drink anything inside.

1

2

3

4

DAY 12

조동사 may / might

혼공기초

This / may not be easy.

이것은 / 쉽지 않을 지도 모른다

혼공개념 001

may는 기본적으로 상대방에게 공손하게 허락을 구할 때 많이 쓰이는 조동사에요. 동사 앞에 쓰여서 '~해도 된다'라는 의미를 가지고 있어요.

May I take your order?

May I use your pencil?

You may go home now.

Bad habits may harm us.

혼공개념 002

may는 상황에 따라 '~일지 모른다'라는 약한 추측을 나타내기도 해요.
might도 마찬가지로 쓰인답니다.

It may snow soon.

Losing may not feel great.

They might be rich.

This expectation might be wrong.

개념확인문제 001 다음 우리말에 맞게 영작한 것을 고르시오.

1 이것은 쉽지 않을 지도 모른다.

① This may be easy.
② This may not be easy.

2 나쁜 습관은 우리에게 해를 끼칠지도 모른다.

① Bad habits may harm us.
② Bad habits may harms us.

3 진다는 것은 기분이 좋지 않을 지도 모른다.

① Losing may not feel great.
② Losing not may feel great.

개념확인문제 002 다음 우리말에 맞게 순서를 바로잡아 영작하시오.

might / expectation / be / This / wrong	이 기대는 잘못된 것일지도 모른다.
➜	

혼공연습

A 다음 문장의 밑줄 친 부분을 보기 처럼 다시 쓰시오.

보기
You ask him anything.
may ask

1 I go shopping tomorrow.

___

2 It is true.

___

3 He calls me back.

___

B 괄호 안의 단어들을 순서에 맞게 써서 문장을 완성하시오.

1 You (any moment | go | may | there | at).
→ You ___.

2 They (not | be | children | might).
→ They ___.

3 He (that | action movie | see | new | might).
→ He ___.

C 다음 문장을 우리말로 해석하시오.

1 You / may not like to wear / a bike helmet.
→

2 You / may not want to go hiking / with your parents.
→

혼공완성

A 사진을 보고 주어진 단어들의 순서를 바로잡아 문장을 완성하시오.

1

fun | may | The ad | look

2
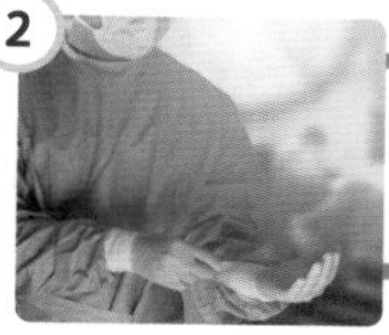

clothes | An emergency room | wear | may | doctor | special

B 주어진 단어들의 순서를 바로잡아 문장을 완성하시오.

1 the rumors | might | bad | Mr. Kim | feel | because of

→

2 repeat | may | many | the behavior | times | You

→

3 may | white coat | have | a negative effect | A doctor's

→

C 다음은 TV 광고에 대한 보고서의 마지막 부분이다. 우리말 해석과 단어를 참고하여 빈칸을 적절히 채우시오.

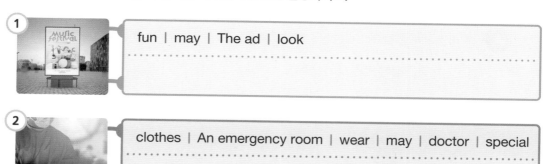

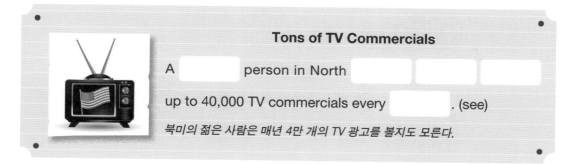

Tons of TV Commercials

A ______ person in North ______ ______ ______ up to 40,000 TV commercials every ______. (see)

북미의 젊은 사람은 매년 4만 개의 TV 광고를 볼지도 모른다.

혼공복습

A 우리말 의미를 참고하여 빈칸을 알맞게 채우시오.

잘 모르겠다면 ···› 83페이지로

1 이것은 쉽지 않을 지도 모른다.

This may ______ be ______.

2 나쁜 습관은 우리에게 해를 끼칠지도 모른다.

Bad ______ may ______ us.

3 진다는 것은 기분이 좋지 않을 지도 모른다.

______ may not ______ great.

4 이 기대는 잘못된 것일지도 모른다.

This ______ might be ______.

B 다음 우리말에 맞게 순서를 바로잡아 영작하시오.

잘 모르겠다면 ···› 84페이지로

1 그것은 사실일지도 모른다.
true | be | may | it

➜

2 그는 나에게 다시 전화걸지도 모른다.
back | may | he | me | call

➜

3 너는 언제든 거기에 가도 된다.
any moment | go | may | there | at | you

➜

4 그는 저 새로나온 액션 영화를 볼지도 모른다.
that | action movie | see | he | new | might

➜

C 주어진 단어들의 순서를 바로잡아 문장을 완성하시오.

잘 모르겠다면 ⋯ 85페이지로

1 to wear | may | not | like | you | a bike helmet

➜

2 with your parents | you | may | not | to go hiking | want

➜

3 clothes | an emergency room | wear | may | doctor | special

➜

4 the rumors | might | bad | Mr. Kim | feel | because of

➜

5 repeat | may | many | the behavior | times | you

➜

D 다음 ❶~❹의 우리말 뜻을 적으시오.

잘 모르겠다면 ⋯ 85페이지로

❶ May I take your order?
❷ The ad may look fun.
❸ A doctor's white coat may have a negative effect.
❹ A young person in North America may see up to 40,000 TV commercials every year.

1

2

3

4

DAY 13

조동사 should / must

혼공기초

We / should take care of them.

우리는 / 그들을 돌봐야 한다

혼공개념 001

좋은 거니까, 바람직한 거니까 '~해야 한다'라고 할 때 **should**를 써요. 조동사니까 동사 앞에 쓰고, 동사는 **s**, **es**, **ed**를 붙이지 않는 '동사원형'을 써야 한다는 것을 잊지 마세요.

We should also wash our hands often.

We should keep rivers clean.

You should go there sometime.

We should be ready for the final exams.

혼공개념 002

반드시 '~해야 한다'는 강한 의무를 말할 때는 **must**를 써요. **have to(has to)**로 대신 쓸 수도 있어요. 또한 상황에 따라서 **must**가 '~인 것이 틀림없다'는 강한 추측을 나타내기도 한답니다.

You must(have to) report a fire.

You must(have to) come to school on time.

It must be true.

He must be thirsty after running.

개념확인문제 001 다음 우리말에 맞게 영작한 것을 고르시오.

1 우리는 그들을 돌봐야 한다.

① We should take care of them.
② We shouldn't take care of them.

2 우리는 기말고사에 준비되어 있어야 한다.

① We should ready be for the final exams.
② We should be ready for the final exams.

3 너는 학교에 제때에 와야 한다.

① You must not come to school on time.
② You have to come to school on time.

개념확인문제 002 다음 우리말에 맞게 순서를 바로잡아 영작하시오.

after running / must / be / He / thirsty	그는 달리기를 한 후에 목이 마른 것이 틀림없다.
➜	

혼공연습

A 다음 문장의 밑줄 친 부분을 보기처럼 다시 쓰시오.

보기 You must clean your room.
have to clean

1 I must do my homework.
____

2 He must wear a mask.
____

3 She must be home by ten o'clock.
____

B 괄호 안의 단어들을 순서에 맞게 써서 문장을 완성하시오.

1 You (the room | food | not | must | eat | in).
→ You _______________.

2 You (be | to | should | polite | others).
→ You _______________.

3 You (to | have | your | room | clean).
→ You _______________.

C 다음 문장을 우리말로 해석하시오.

1 We / must have breakfast first.
→

2 He / must be a good teacher.
→

혼공완성

A 사진을 보고 주어진 단어들의 순서를 바로잡아 문장을 완성하시오.

1 

be | must | It | enjoyable

2 

shouldn't | a bike | You | here | ride

B 주어진 단어들의 순서를 바로잡아 문장을 완성하시오.

1 a superhero | must | She | be

➜

2 tonight | must | go | You | early | to bed

➜

3 should | We | the rules | follow | of the museum

➜

C 다음 안내문을 읽고 손을 씻어야 하는 경우 3가지를 우리말로 쓰시오.

You should wash your hands:

- after arriving home
- after coughing
- before eating food

① ______________________

② ______________________

③ ______________________

혼공복습

A 우리말 의미를 참고하여 빈칸을 알맞게 채우시오.

잘 모르겠다면 ···› 89페이지로

1 우리는 그들을 돌봐야 한다.

We should ______ care of ______ .

2 우리는 기말고사에 준비되어 있어야 한다.

We should ______ ready for the ______ exams.

3 너는 학교에 제때에 와야 한다.

You ______ to come to school ______ time.

4 그는 달리기를 한 후에 목이 마른 것이 틀림없다.

He ______ be ______ after running.

B 다음 우리말에 맞게 순서를 바로잡아 영작하시오.

잘 모르겠다면 ···› 90페이지로

1 그녀는 10시 정각까지 집에 돌아와야 한다.
she | by ten o'clock | be | must | home

➜

2 너는 방에서 음식을 먹어서는 안된다.
the room | food | not | must | you | eat | in

➜

3 너는 다른 사람들에게 공손해야 한다.
be | you | to | should | polite | others

➜

4 너는 너의 방을 청소해야 한다.
to | have | you | your | room | clean

➜

C 주어진 단어들의 순서를 바로잡아 문장을 완성하시오.

잘 모르겠다면 ···› 91페이지로

1 be | must | it | enjoyable

➜

2 shouldn't | a bike | you | here | ride

➜

3 a superhero | must | she | be

➜

4 tonight | must | go | you | early | to bed

➜

5 should | we | the rules | follow | of the museum

➜

D 다음 ❶~❹의 우리말 뜻을 적으시오.

잘 모르겠다면 ···› 91페이지로

❶ He must be a good teacher.
❷ You should wash your hands after arriving home.
❸ You should wash your hands after coughing.
❹ You should wash your hands before eating food.

1

2

3

4

기타 조동사

혼공기초

People / used to pay in gold.
사람들은 / 금으로 지불하곤 했다

혼공개념 001

'~하곤 했다'라는 의미로 예전에는 반복적으로 했었지만 지금은 더 이상 하지 않는 '과거의 습관'을 나타낼 때 **used to**와 **would**를 써요. 특히 **used to**는 **'There used to be~'**의 형태로 '~가 있었지만 지금은 없다'라는 과거의 상태도 나타낼 수 있어요.

I used to share a bedroom with my sister. 과거의 습관

Harry used to go to our school. 과거의 습관

My dad would go snowboarding. 과거의 습관

There used to be a cinema here. 과거의 상태

혼공개념 002

'~하는 게 낫다'라는 의미로 상대방이 꼭 그래야 한다는 강한 충고를 할 때 **had better**를 써요.

You had better travel to Moscow tomorrow.

You had better not use your smartphone during class.

We had better leave for Gwangju now.

We had better not tell Mr. Kim about the broken vase.

개념확인문제 001 다음 우리말에 맞게 영작한 것을 고르시오.

1 사람들은 금으로 지불하곤 했다.

① People used to pay in gold.
② People had better pay in gold.

2 Harry는 우리 학교에 다녔었다.

① Harry used to go to our school.
② Harry used to going to our school.

3 예전에 여기에 영화 극장이 있었다.

① There would be a cinema here.
② There used to be a cinema here.

개념확인문제 002 다음 우리말에 맞게 순서를 바로잡아 영작하시오.

not / your smartphone / use / had better / during class / You	너는 수업 중에 스마트폰을 사용하지 않는 게 낫다.
➜	

혼공연습

A 다음 문장의 밑줄 친 부분을 보고 보기 처럼 '과거의 습관', '과거의 상태' 중 하나를 쓰시오.

보기 He would clean your room.
과거의 습관

1 I used to keep a diary.

____

2 There used to be a post office here.

____

3 My grandparents would get up early in the morning.

____

B 괄호 안의 단어들을 순서에 맞게 써서 문장을 완성하시오.

1 The hotel (a park | to | used | be).

→ The hotel ______________________.

2 He (be | weak | very | to | used).

→ He ______________________.

3 Bill (on weekends | his | visit | grandparents | would).

→ Bill ______________________.

C 다음 문장을 우리말로 해석하시오.

1 My father / used to tell us / bedtime stories.

→

2 You / had better eat / more fruits and vegetables.

→

혼공완성

A 사진을 보고 주어진 단어들의 순서를 바로잡아 문장을 완성하시오.

1

swords | fight | would | with | People

2

at the circus | I | to | like | used | the clowns

B 주어진 단어들의 순서를 바로잡아 문장을 완성하시오.

1 crowded | The town | be | very | used | to

➜

2 better | You | your coat | had | put on

➜

3 next | used | Mrs. Brown | live | door | to

➜

C 다음 글에서 나오는 'I'에 대한 내용과 일치하도록 빈칸을 우리말로 알맞게 채우시오.

I used to live in London.
I used to love chocolate.
I used to be blonde.
I used to walk to school every day.

1 예전에 ________에 살았었다.

2 ________을 좋아했었다.

3 머리색이 ________이었다.

4 매일 학교에 ________ 다녔었다.

혼공복습

A 우리말 의미를 참고하여 빈칸을 알맞게 채우시오.

잘 모르겠다면 ··· 95페이지로

1. 사람들은 금으로 지불하곤 했다.

   People ______ to ______ in gold.

2. Harry는 우리 학교에 다녔었다.

   Harry used to ______ to our ______ .

3. 예전에 여기에 영화 극장이 있었다.

   ______ used to ______ a cinema here.

4. 너는 수업 중에 스마트폰을 사용하지 않는 게 낫다.

   You had ______ not ______ your smartphone during class.

B 다음 우리말에 맞게 순서를 바로잡아 영작하시오.

잘 모르겠다면 ··· 96페이지로

1. 나는 일기를 쓰곤 했다.
   a diary | I | keep | used to

   ➜

2. 여기에 우체국이 있었다.
   used to | there | a post office | here | be

   ➜

3. 그 호텔은 예전에 공원이었다.
   a park | to | used | be | the hotel

   ➜

4. Bill은 주말에 그의 조부모님들을 방문하곤 했다.
   on weekends | his | visit | Bill | grandparents | would

   ➜

C 주어진 단어들의 순서를 바로잡아 문장을 완성하시오.

잘 모르겠다면 ···› 97페이지로

1 swords | fight | would | with | people

→

2 at the circus | I | to | like | used | the clowns

→

3 crowded | the town | be | very | used | to

→

4 better | you | your coat | had | put on

→

5 next | used | Mrs. Brown | live | door | to

→

D 다음 ❶~❹의 우리말 뜻을 적으시오.

잘 모르겠다면 ···› 97페이지로

❶ I used to live in London.
❷ I used to love chocolate.
❸ I used to be blonde.
❹ I used to walk to school every day.

1

2

3

4

DAY 15

조동사 + have + p.p.

혼공기초

I / should have arrived earlier.

나는 / 더 일찍 도착했어야 하는데

혼공개념 001

조동사 **must** / **could** / **may**(**might**) / **can't** + **have** + **p.p.**로 과거에 대한 추측을 표현할 수 있어요. 각각, '~했던 것이 분명하다', '~했을 수도 있다', '~했을 지도 모른다', '~했을 리가 없다'의 의미로 해석해요.

He must have found my attitude annoying.

Someone could have been hurt.

They may have heard of BTS.

Ms. Park can't have arrived already.

혼공개념 002

should + have + p.p.를 써서 '~했어야 하는데'라는 과거에 하지 않은 것을 후회하는 표현을 할 수 있어요.

You should have kept the door locked.

We should have done the project my way.

She should have finished it by the middle of the week.

They shouldn't have made such a decision.

개념확인문제 001

다음 우리말에 맞게 영작한 것을 고르시오.

1 나는 더 일찍 도착했어야 하는데.

① I should have arrived earlier.
② I must have arrived earlier.

2 어떤 사람은 다쳤을 수도 있다.

① Someone can't have been hurt.
② Someone could have been hurt.

3 너는 그 문을 잠갔어야 하는데.

① You should keep the door locked.
② You should have kept the door locked.

개념확인문제 002

다음 우리말에 맞게 순서를 바로잡아 영작하시오.

should / of the week / have / it / She / by the middle / finished	그녀는 그것을 그 주 중간까지 끝마쳤어야 하는데.
➜	

혼공연습

A 다음 문장의 밑줄 친 부분을 보기 처럼 다시 쓰시오.

보기
I lost my smartphone. (must)
must have lost

1 She left her keys behind. (may)

____

2 Someone entered my room. (must)

____

3 We won without you. (could)

____

B 괄호 안의 단어들을 순서에 맞게 써서 문장을 완성하시오.

1 He (from | fallen | have | the roof | must).
→ He ______________________.

2 The rain (stopped | might | have).
→ The rain ______________________.

3 It (have | can't | his | been | car).
→ It ______________________.

C 다음 문장을 우리말로 해석하시오.

1 The accident / could have been worse.
→

2 You / should have come / to the school festival.
→

혼공완성

A 사진을 보고 주어진 단어들의 순서를 바로잡아 문장을 완성하시오.

1

He | have | all that noise | slept | through | can't

2

him | might | have | The pills | helped

B 주어진 단어들의 순서를 바로잡아 문장을 완성하시오.

1 missed | have | could | the train | They

➜

2 of Saturn's rings | the riddle | The scientist | have | may | solved

➜

3 must | your | disturbed | birthday party | He | have

➜

C 다음은 탐정의 조사 내용이다. 보기에 주어진 단어를 한 번씩 써서 빈칸을 채우시오(필요할 경우 동사의 형태를 바꿀 수 있음).

Someone must have left the __________ open by mistake.

Someone must have __________ the plate.

Someone might have __________ the thief.

Someone could have spilled some __________ on the table.

보기 coffee see gate break

혼공복습

A 우리말 의미를 참고하여 빈칸을 알맞게 채우시오.

잘 모르겠다면 ···› 101페이지로

1 나는 더 일찍 도착했어야 하는데.

I ______ have ______ earlier.

2 어떤 사람은 다쳤을 수도 있다.

Someone could have ______ ______.

3 너는 그 문을 잠갔어야 하는데.

You ______ have kept the ______ locked.

4 그녀는 그것을 그 주 중간까지 끝마쳤어야 하는데.

She should have ______ it by the ______ of the week.

B 다음 우리말에 맞게 순서를 바로잡아 영작하시오.

잘 모르겠다면 ···› 102페이지로

1 어떤 사람이 내 방에 들어온 것이 분명하다.
must | someone | entered | have | my room

➜

2 우리는 너 없이 이겼을 수도 있어.
could | we | won | have | without you

➜

3 그는 지붕에서 떨어진 것이 분명하다.
from | fallen | have | he | the roof | must

➜

4 비가 멎었을지도 모른다.
stopped | might | the rain | have

➜

C 주어진 단어들의 순서를 바로잡아 문장을 완성하시오.

잘 모르겠다면 ···› 103페이지로

1 been | could | have | the accident | worse

➜

2 he | have | all that noise | slept | through | can't

➜

3 him | might | have | the pills | helped

➜

4 missed | have | could | the train | they

➜

5 of Saturn's rings | the riddle | the scientist | have | may | solved

➜

D 다음 ❶~❹의 우리말 뜻을 적으시오.

잘 모르겠다면 ···› 103페이지로

❶ Someone must have left the gate open by mistake.
❷ Someone must have broken the plate.
❸ Someone might have seen the thief.
❹ Someone could have spilled some coffee on the table.

1

2

3

4

Part 4

전달 방향 이해하기

수동태

- Day 16 Gold is found in the mine.
- Day 17 It was built about 500 years ago.
- Day 18 A new stadium will be built here.
- Day 19 They are interested in board games.
- Day 20 The lion is known by its claws.

DAY 16 능동태 / 수동태

혼공기초

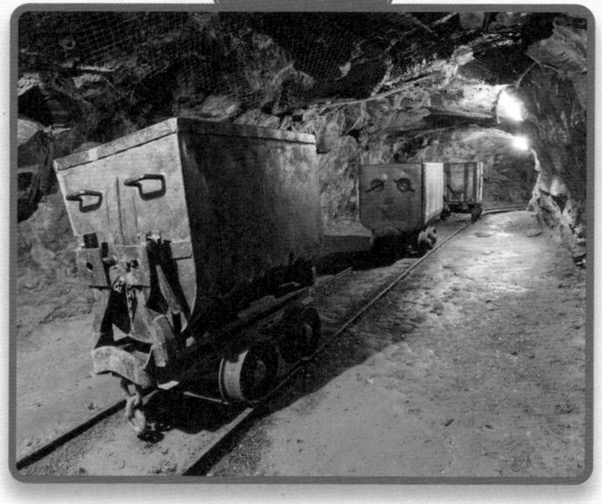

Gold / is found in the mine.
금이 / 그 광산에서 발견된다

혼공개념 001

주어가 직접 동작을 하는 것을 능동태라고 하고, '~은/는/이/가 ~ 하다'라고 해석해요.

Both children and adults love the character.

A lot of kids still sing his song.

People read the Harry Potter books in many different languages.

They deliver fresh milk from the farm every morning.

혼공개념 002

주어가 동작을 받는 것을 수동태라고 하고, **be + p.p.**로 동작 부분을 표현해요. 만약 행위자를 나타내야 할 경우에는 마지막에 **'by + 행위자'**를 붙여 쓰고, 행위자를 나타낼 필요가 없는 경우에는 생략해요.

The character is loved by both children and adults.

His song is still sung by a lot of kids.

The Harry Potter books are read in many different languages. 행위자 생략

Fresh milk is delivered from the farm every morning. 행위자 생략

개념확인문제 001 다음 우리말에 맞게 영작한 것을 고르시오.

1 금이 그 광산에서 발견된다.

① Gold finds in the mine.
② Gold is found in the mine.

2 많은 아이들이 여전히 그의 노래를 부른다.

① A lot of kids still sing his song.
② A lot of kids still is sung his song.

3 해리포터 책들은 많은 다른 언어로 읽혀진다.

① The Harry Potter books are read in many different languages.
② The Harry Potter books are reading in many different languages.

개념확인문제 002 다음 우리말에 맞게 순서를 바로잡아 영작하시오.

every morning / delivered / Fresh / is / milk / from the farm	신선한 우유가 농장에서 매일 아침 배달된다.

➜

혼공연습

A 보기 처럼 주어진 문장을 수동태로 바꿀 때 빈칸을 적절히 채우시오.

> 보기
> My dad waters the plant every morning.
> → The plant is watered by my dad every morning.

1 German students visit our school.
→ Our school ________ ________ by German students.

2 We cook every meal from fresh food.
→ Every meal ________ ________ from fresh food.

3 My younger brother causes big problems.
→ Big problems ________ ________ by my younger brother.

B 괄호 안의 단어들을 순서에 맞게 써서 문장을 완성하시오.

1 English (used | is | over | all | the world).
→ English ________________.

2 The problems (never | again | mentioned | are).
→ The problems ________________.

3 Many workers (the company | every year | fired | by | are).
→ Many workers ________________.

C 다음 문장을 우리말로 해석하시오.

1 The forests / are destroyed / by humans.
→

2 The story / is not written / in French.
→

혼공완성

A 사진을 보고 주어진 단어들의 순서를 바로잡아 문장을 완성하시오.

1

my | taken | A lot of | uncle | photos | by | are

2

two | built | by | The treehouse | is | famous builders

B 주어진 단어들의 순서를 바로잡아 문장을 완성하시오.

1 is | The jazz | held | June | festival | in

➜

2 actors | by | invited | Popular | are | the government

➜

3 by | character | is | The main | Scarlett Johansson | played

➜

C 다음은 세계적인 사원 앙코르 와트에 대해 조사한 내용이다. 주어진 동사를 활용하여 빈칸을 채우시오 (필요할 경우 동사의 형태를 바꿀 수 있음).

Angkor Wat

Angkor Wat is ______ in northwest Cambodia. (locate)

Angkor Wat is ______ by a lot of tourists every year. (visit)

혼공복습

A 우리말 의미를 참고하여 빈칸을 알맞게 채우시오.

잘 모르겠다면 ···› 109페이지로

1 금이 그 광산에서 발견된다.

Gold is ______ in the ______.

2 많은 아이들이 여전히 그의 노래를 부른다.

A lot of kids still ______ his ______.

3 해리포터 책들은 많은 다른 언어로 읽혀진다.

The Harry Potter books are ______ in many different ______.

4 신선한 우유가 농장에서 매일 아침 배달된다.

Fresh milk is ______ from the ______ every morning.

B 다음 우리말에 맞게 순서를 바로잡아 영작하시오.

잘 모르겠다면 ···› 110페이지로

1 영어는 전 세계에서 사용된다.
used | is | over | all | English | the world

➜

2 많은 노동자들이 매년 그 회사에 의해 해고된다.
workers | fired | by | many | the company | are | every year

➜

3 숲은 인간에 의해 파괴된다.
by | are | the forests | destroyed | humans

➜

4 그 이야기는 프랑스어로 쓰여지지 않는다.
in French | is | not | the story | written

➜

C 주어진 단어들의 순서를 바로잡아 문장을 완성하시오.

잘 모르겠다면 ···› 111페이지로

1 my | taken | a lot of | uncle | photos | by | are

➜

2 two | built | by | the treehouse | is | famous builders

➜

3 is | the jazz | held | June | festival | in

➜

4 actors | by | invited | popular | are | the government

➜

5 by | character | is | the main | Scarlett Johansson | played

➜

D 다음 ❶~❹의 우리말 뜻을 적으시오.

잘 모르겠다면 ···› 111페이지로

❶ Every meal is cooked from fresh food.
❷ Big problems are caused by my younger brother.
❸ Angkor Wat is located in northwest Cambodia.
❹ Angkor Wat is visited by a lot of tourists every year.

1

2

3

4

DAY 17 수동태의 시제 1

혼공기초

It / was built about 500 years ago.

그것은 / 약 500년 전에 지어졌다

혼공개념 001

수동태의 **be**동사 부분을 **was**, **were**로 쓰면 과거 시제를 나타낼 수 있어요.

He was named after his uncle.

A new car was bought by my parents last year.

One hundred guests were invited to the wedding.

The towns were built close to rivers.

혼공개념 002

be + being + p.p.로 수동태의 진행형을 표현할 수 있어요. 이때 주어와 시제를 잘 생각해서 **am, is, are** 또는 **was, were** 중 알맞은 **be**동사를 써야 해요.

I am being punished for three months.

These trees are being grown for timber.

I was being watched.

Drinks were being sold from the shelf.

개념확인문제 001 다음 우리말에 맞게 영작한 것을 고르시오.

1 그것은 약 500년 전에 지어졌다.

① It is built about 500 years ago.
② It was built about 500 years ago.

2 그는 그의 삼촌을 따라서 이름 지어졌다.

① He was named after his uncle.
② He were named after his uncle.

3 나는 세 달 동안 벌을 받고 있는 중이다.

① I am punished being for three months.
② I am being punished for three months.

개념확인문제 002 다음 우리말에 맞게 순서를 바로잡아 영작하시오.

are / These trees / grown / for timber / being	이 나무들은 목재를 위해 키워지는 중이다.
➜	

혼공연습

A 보기 처럼 밑줄 친 부분을 과거수동태로 바꾸시오.

보기 The house builds on a mountain.
was built

1. A hotel room prepares for them.
➜ A hotel room ____________ for them.

2. Our kitchen cleans every day.
➜ Our kitchen ____________ every day.

3. The fire puts out by the fire fighters.
➜ The fire ____________ by the fire fighters.

B 괄호 안의 단어들을 순서에 맞게 써서 문장을 완성하시오.

1. Children (at PIZZA LOCA | given | a toy | were).
➜ Children .

2. The plants (watered | were | my | by | mother).
➜ The plants .

3. The tests (by | taken | the students | were).
➜ The tests .

C 다음 문장을 우리말로 해석하시오.

1. Tickets / were being sold / for $300.
➜

2. Too much waste / is being dumped / at sea.
➜

혼공완성

A 사진을 보고 주어진 단어들의 순서를 바로잡아 문장을 완성하시오.

1 

is | Water | being | on the stove | boiled

2 

was | The cake | in the oven | baked

B 주어진 단어들의 순서를 바로잡아 문장을 완성하시오.

1 in our area | A beauty salon | being | is | run

→

2 completed | The Eiffel Tower | in 1889 | was

→

3 being | were | Two women | by the police | interviewed

→

C 주어진 단어를 활용하여 과거에 일어난 사실을 완성하시오(필요할 경우 단어를 추가할 수 있음).

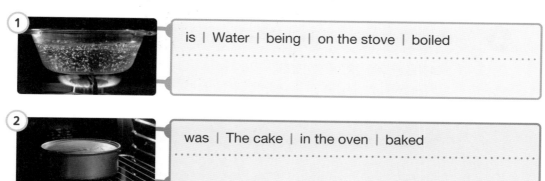

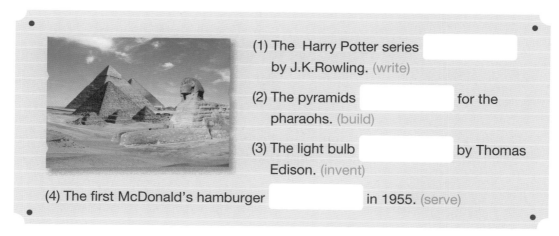

(1) The Harry Potter series ________ by J.K.Rowling. (write)

(2) The pyramids ________ for the pharaohs. (build)

(3) The light bulb ________ by Thomas Edison. (invent)

(4) The first McDonald's hamburger ________ in 1955. (serve)

혼공복습

A 우리말 의미를 참고하여 빈칸을 알맞게 채우시오.

잘 모르겠다면 ···› 115페이지로

1 그것은 약 500년 전에 지어졌다.

It ______ ______ about 500 years ago.

2 그는 그의 삼촌을 따라서 이름 지어졌다.

He was ______ after his ______ .

3 나는 세 달 동안 벌을 받고 있는 중이다.

I am ______ ______ for three months.

4 이 나무들은 목재를 위해 키워지는 중이다.

These ______ are being ______ for timber.

B 다음 우리말에 맞게 순서를 바로잡아 영작하시오.

잘 모르겠다면 ···› 116페이지로

1 한 호텔 방이 그들을 위해 준비되었다.
was | a hotel room | for them | prepared

➜

2 그 화재는 그 소방관들에 의해 진화되었다.
the fire fighters | the fire | put out | was | by

➜

3 그 시험들은 그 학생들에 의해 치러졌다.
the students | the tests | taken | were | by

➜

4 표들은 300달러에 팔리고 있는 중이었다
for $300 | were | being | tickets | sold

➜

C 주어진 단어들의 순서를 바로잡아 문장을 완성하시오.

잘 모르겠다면 …› 117페이지로

1 too much | being | waste | is | at sea | dumped

➜

2 is | water | being | on the stove | boiled

➜

3 was | the cake | in the oven | baked

➜

4 in our area | a beauty salon | being | is | run

➜

5 being | were | two women | by the police | interviewed

➜

D 다음 ❶~❹의 우리말 뜻을 적으시오.

잘 모르겠다면 …› 117페이지로

❶ The Harry Potter series was written by J.K.Rowling.
❷ The pyramids were built for the pharaohs.
❸ The light bulb was invented by Thomas Edison.
❹ The first McDonald's hamburger was served in 1955.

1

2

3

4

DAY 18

수동태의 시제 2

혼공기초

A new stadium /
will be built here.
새 경기장이 / 여기에 지어질 것이다

혼공개념 001

조동사 + **be** + **p.p.**를 사용하여 미래, 의무, 추측 등을 수동태와 같이 사용할 수 있어요. 조동사 다음에는 반드시 동사원형인 **be**를 써야 해요.

Coffee will be made by my dad every morning.

The company should be run by Dr. Ken.

The ballpark can be emptied in five minutes.

The knife must be sharpened on a stone.

혼공개념 002

현재완료 역시 수동표현으로 나타낼 수 있어요. **'have(has) + been + p.p.'** 로 쓰고 '~되어왔다', '~되어졌다'라는 의미를 가지고 있어요.

The thief has been caught by a brave man.

The office has already been cleaned.

A letter has just been delivered.

The river has just been crossed by the runners.

개념확인문제 001 다음 우리말에 맞게 영작한 것을 고르시오.

1 새 경기장이 여기에 지어질 것이다.

① A new stadium will build here.
② A new stadium will be built here.

2 커피는 내 아빠에 의해 매일 아침 만들어 질 것이다.

① Coffee will be made by my dad every morning.
② Coffee must be made by my dad every morning.

3 그 야구장은 5분 뒤에 비워질 수 있다.

① The ballpark can emptied be in five minutes.
② The ballpark can be emptied in five minutes.

개념확인문제 002 다음 우리말에 맞게 순서를 바로잡아 영작하시오.

already / cleaned / has / The office / been	사무실은 이미 청소되어졌다.
➜	

혼공연습

A 다음 문장을 보기 처럼 주어진 지시에 맞춰서 바꾸시오.

보기
The rooms are booked tomorrow. (미래)
➡ The rooms will be booked tomorrow.

1 The bone is eaten by the dog. (가능)
➡ The bone ____________ by the dog.

2 Coke is produced by The Coca Cola Company. (강한의무)
➡ Coke ____________ by The Coca Cola Company.

3 The movie is directed by Christopher Nolan. (약한추측)
➡ The movie ____________ by Christopher Nolan.

B 괄호 안의 단어들을 순서에 맞게 써서 문장을 완성하시오.

1 Lunch (my father | been | has | by | cooked | on Sundays).
➡ Lunch ____________ .

2 K-pop (will | more | enjoyed | in | be | countries).
➡ K-pop ____________ .

3 The walls (by | been | have | painted | the students).
➡ The walls ____________ .

C 다음 문장을 우리말로 해석하시오.

1 The plants / have been watered / since last month.
➡

2 A new cookbook / will be released / next year.
➡

혼공완성

A 사진을 보고 주어진 단어들의 순서를 바로잡아 문장을 완성하시오.

1 

has | all over the world | been | Monopoly | played

2 

be | the meal | must | All the dishes | washed | after

B 주어진 단어들의 순서를 바로잡아 문장을 완성하시오.

1 in the price | be | All drinks | may | included

→

2 has | by | been | visited | The national park | many tourists

→

3 have | must | The match | finished | been

→

C 다음은 **Jimmy**네 집의 규칙이다. 주어진 단어를 의미에 맞게 변형해서 쓰시오(변형할 필요가 없다면 그대로 쓸 수 있음).

(1) Dirty clothes should be ______ at home. (wash)

(2) At least a book a day should be ______. (read)

(3) Homework should be ______ in the morning. (do)

(4) Jimmy's room should be ______ every day. (clean)

혼공복습

A 우리말 의미를 참고하여 빈칸을 알맞게 채우시오.

잘 모르겠다면 ⋯ 121페이지로

1. 새 경기장이 여기에 지어질 것이다.

   A new stadium ______ be ______ here.

2. 커피는 내 아빠에 의해 매일 아침 만들어 질 것이다.

   Coffee ______ be ______ by my dad every morning.

3. 그 야구장은 5분 뒤에 비워질 수 있다.

   The ballpark ______ be ______ in five minutes.

4. 사무실은 이미 청소되어졌다.

   The office ______ already been ______ .

B 다음 우리말에 맞게 순서를 바로잡아 영작하시오.

잘 모르겠다면 ⋯ 122페이지로

1. 그 영화는 Christopher Nolan에 의해 연출되어질 지도 모른다.

   may | directed | be | the movie | by Christopher Nolan

   ➜

2. 점심은 일요일마다 내 아버지에 의해서 요리되어왔다.

   my father | been | has | by | cooked | lunch | on Sundays

   ➜

3. 그 식물들은 지난 달 이후로 물이 뿌려져 왔다.

   have | the plants | been | since | watered | last month

   ➜

4. 새로운 요리책이 내년에 발간될 것이다.

   a new | released | next year | will | cookbook | be

   ➜

C 주어진 단어들의 순서를 바로잡아 문장을 완성하시오.

잘 모르겠다면 ···› 123페이지로

1 has | all over the world | been | Monopoly | played

➜

2 be | the meal | must | all the dishes | washed | after

➜

3 in the price | be | all drinks | may | included

➜

4 has | by | been | visited | the national park | many tourists

➜

5 have | must | the match | finished | been

➜

D 다음 ❶~❹의 우리말 뜻을 적으시오.

잘 모르겠다면 ···› 123페이지로

❶ Dirty clothes should be washed at home.
❷ At least a book a day should be read.
❸ Homework should be done in the morning.
❹ Jimmy's room should be cleaned every day.

1

2

3

4

DAY 19 수동태의 관용표현 1

혼공기초

They / are interested in board games.

그들은 / 보드 게임에 관심이 있다

혼공개념 001

수동태로 감정을 표현할 때 **by** 이외의 다른 전치사가 사용되기도 해요. **be interested in**(~에 관심이 있다), **be satisfied with**(~에 만족하다), **be surprised at[by]**(~에 놀라다), **be disappointed with[by]**(~에 실망하다)가 대표적인 표현이니 기억하세요.

Mr. Sun is interested in learning new languages.

I am satisfied with my life.

He was surprised by my questions.

The fishermen were disappointed with their catch that day.

혼공개념 002

수동태로 상태를 표현할 때도 **by** 이외의 다른 전치사가 사용되기도 해요. **be covered with**(~으로 덮여 있다), **be engaged in**(~에 종사하다), **be filled with**(~로 가득 차다), **be caught in**(비 따위를 만나다)가 대표적인 표현이니 기억하세요.

The rock was covered with seaweed.

He was engaged in running a small business.

Paul's face was filled with anger.

I was caught in a storm.

개념확인문제 001 다음 우리말에 맞게 영작한 것을 고르시오.

1 그들은 보드 게임에 관심이 있다.

① They are interested in board games.
② They are interested by board games.

2 나는 내 삶에 만족스럽다.

① I am satisfied at my life.
② I am satisfied with my life.

3 그는 작은 사업을 운영하는데 종사하고 있었다.

① He was engaged in running a small business.
② He was engaged by running a small business.

개념확인문제 002 다음 우리말에 맞게 순서를 바로잡아 영작하시오.

filled / face / with / was / Paul's / anger	Paul의 얼굴은 분노로 가득 찼다.

➔

혼공연습

A 보기 에서 알맞은 단어를 찾아 한 번씩 빈칸에 쓰시오.

보기 caught filled disappointed

1 The room was __________ with smoke.

2 He was unfortunately __________ in the shower.

3 He was __________ by his failure.

B 괄호 안의 단어들을 순서에 맞게 써서 문장을 완성하시오.

1 The park (filled | people | was | with).

→ The park __________.

2 The grass (covered | was | with | frost).

→ The grass __________.

3 I (disappointed | by | was | attitude | her).

→ I __________.

C 다음 문장을 우리말로 해석하시오.

1 He / wasn't interested / in growing flowers / in the garden.

→

2 The front of the building / was covered / with ivy.

→

혼공완성

A 사진을 보고 주어진 단어들의 순서를 바로잡아 문장을 완성하시오.

1

were | satisfied | with | the new house | They

2

with | The top | covered | was | snow | of the mountain

B 주어진 단어들의 순서를 바로잡아 문장을 완성하시오.

1 these | results | are | satisfied | We | not | with

→

2 with | was | the sound | filled | The dawn | of birds

→

3 covered | notebook | is | with | Sophie's | stickers

→

C 다음은 Terry가 치른 쪽지 시험의 결과이다. 밑줄 친 단어를 알맞게 고치시오.

Name: Terry Bogard

❶ I'm not satisfied <u>at</u> his answer.
❷ He was deeply interested <u>by</u> yoga.
❸ His face was covered <u>at</u> wrinkles.
❹ The air was filled <u>in</u> the smell of flowers.

1 ________ 2 ________ 3 ________ 4 ________

혼공복습

A 우리말 의미를 참고하여 빈칸을 알맞게 채우시오.

잘 모르겠다면 ···› 127페이지로

1. 그들은 보드 게임에 관심이 있다.
   They are ________ ________ board games.

2. 나는 내 삶에 만족스럽다.
   I am ________ ________ my life.

3. 그는 작은 사업을 운영하는데 종사하고 있었다.
   He was ________ in running a small ________.

4. Paul의 얼굴은 분노로 가득 찼다.
   Paul's face was ________ ________ anger.

B 다음 우리말에 맞게 순서를 바로잡아 영작하시오.

잘 모르겠다면 ···› 128페이지로

1. 그 공원은 사람들로 가득 찼다.
   filled | people | the park | was | with
   ➜

2. 잔디는 서리로 뒤덮여 있었다.
   covered | was | with | the grass | frost
   ➜

3. 나는 그녀의 태도에 실망했다.
   disappointed | by | was | attitude | I | her
   ➜

4. 그는 정원에서 꽃을 키우는 것에 관심이 없었다.
   wasn't | he | in | interested | flowers | in the garden | growing
   ➜

C 주어진 단어들의 순서를 바로잡아 문장을 완성하시오.

잘 모르겠다면 …→ 129페이지로

1. were | satisfied | with | the new house | they

→

2. with | the top | covered | was | snow | of the mountain

→

3. these | results | are | satisfied | we | not | with

→

4. with | was | the sound | filled | the dawn | of birds

→

5. covered | notebook | is | with | Sophie's | stickers

→

D 다음 ❶~❹의 우리말 뜻을 적으시오.

잘 모르겠다면 …→ 129페이지로

❶ I'm not satisfied with his answer.
❷ He was deeply interested in yoga.
❸ His face was covered with wrinkles.
❹ The air was filled with the smell of flowers.

1

2

3

4

DAY 20

수동태의 관용표현 2

혼공기초

The lion / is known by its claws.

사자는 / 그것의 발톱에 의해 알 수 있다

혼공개념 001

be known to(~에게 알려져 있다), **be known as**(~로 알려져 있다), **be known for**(~로 유명하다), **be known by**(~에 의해 알 수 있다) 처럼 관용적으로 쓰이는 표현들을 잘 알아둬야 해요.

The actor is well known to us.

He was known as "Iron Man" to his friends.

Mr. Kim is known for his sense of humor.

A tree is known by its fruit.

혼공개념 002

be known to 다음에 **be**동사나 동사원형이 오는 경우가 있어요. 이럴 때는 '~인 것으로 알려져 있다, ~하는 것으로 알려져 있다'라고 해석하면 된답니다.

Drinking is known to be bad for your health.

He has been known to go shopping by himself.

He has been known to spend all morning in the bathroom.

This chemical is known to be harmful to children.

개념확인문제 001 다음 우리말에 맞게 영작한 것을 고르시오.

1 사자는 그것의 발톱에 의해 알 수 있다.

① The lion is known by its claws.
② The lion is known for its claws.

2 그는 그의 친구들에게 아이언 맨으로 알려져 있었다.

① He was known as "Iron Man" to his friends.
② He was known by "Iron Man" to his friends.

3 김 선생님은 그의 유머 감각으로 유명하다.

① Mr. Kim is known as his sense of humor.
② Mr. Kim is known for his sense of humor.

개념확인문제 002 다음 우리말에 맞게 순서를 바로잡아 영작하시오.

be / is / known / bad / Drinking / to / for / your health	음주는 당신의 건강에 나쁜 것으로 알려져 있다.

➜

혼공연습

A 보기 에서 알맞은 단어를 찾아 한 번씩 빈칸에 쓰시오.

보기	as	by	to

1. A man is known __________ his friends.
2. The truth was known __________ no one.
3. She was known __________ a great beauty.

B 괄호 안의 단어들을 순서에 맞게 써서 문장을 완성하시오.

1. She (to | known | kindness | all | for | was | her).
   ➜ She ____________________.
2. This man (to | is | the police | known).
   ➜ This man ____________________.
3. He (for | is | his | known | looks | good).
   ➜ He ____________________.

C 다음 문장을 우리말로 해석하시오.

1. A man / is known / by the company / he keeps.
   ➜
2. Smoking / is known / to increase a person's risk / of developing lung cancer.
   ➜

혼공완성

A 사진을 보고 주어진 단어들의 순서를 바로잡아 문장을 완성하시오.

1

driver | known | as | was | a very | David | fast

2

for | It | its | handicraft | is | products | known

B 주어진 단어들의 순서를 바로잡아 문장을 완성하시오.

1 of New York | This area | known | is | Soho | as

→

2 songs | known | its | may | be | A bird | by

→

3 people | are | The French | as | known | a food-loving

→

C 다음 어구를 의미에 맞도록 적절히 연결하시오.

❶ Bong Joon-ho is known for •
❷ The Curies are best known for •
❸ South Africa is well known for •
❹ Sodium chloride is known as •

• salt.
• its diamond mines.
• discovering radium.
• his movie, *Parasite*.

혼공복습

A 우리말 의미를 참고하여 빈칸을 알맞게 채우시오.

잘 모르겠다면 ···→ 133페이지로

1. 사자는 그것의 발톱에 의해 알 수 있다.

   The lion is ______ ______ its claws.

2. 그는 그의 친구들에게 아이언 맨으로 알려져 있었다.

   He ______ known ______ "Iron Man" to his friends.

3. 김 선생님은 그의 유머 감각으로 유명하다.

   Mr. Kim is ______ for his ______ of humor.

4. 음주는 당신의 건강에 나쁜 것으로 알려져 있다.

   Drinking is ______ to be bad for your ______.

B 다음 우리말에 맞게 순서를 바로잡아 영작하시오.

잘 모르겠다면 ···→ 134페이지로

1. 그녀는 그녀의 친절로 모두에게 유명했다.

   to | known | kindness | she | all | for | was | her

   →

2. 이 남자는 경찰에게 알려져 있다.

   to | is | the police | this | known | man

   →

3. 그는 그의 잘생긴 외모로 유명하다.

   for | is | his | known | he | looks | good

   →

4. 흡연은 한 사람의 폐암을 생기게 하는 위험을 높이는 것으로 알려져 있다.

   is | lung cancer | known | to increase | smoking | of developing | a person's risk

   →

C 주어진 단어들의 순서를 바로잡아 문장을 완성하시오.

잘 모르겠다면 ... 135페이지로

1 driver | known | as | was | a very | David | fast

→

2 for | it | its | handicraft | is | products | known

→

3 of New York | this area | known | is | Soho | as

→

4 songs | known | its | may | be | a bird | by

→

5 people | are | the French | as | known | a food-loving

→

D 다음 ❶~❹의 우리말 뜻을 적으시오.

잘 모르겠다면 ... 135페이지로

❶ Bong Joon-ho is known for his movie, *Parasite*.
❷ The Curies are best known for discovering radium.
❸ South Africa is well known for its diamond mines.
❹ Sodium chloride is known as salt.

1

2

3

4

Part 5

Special 60문장

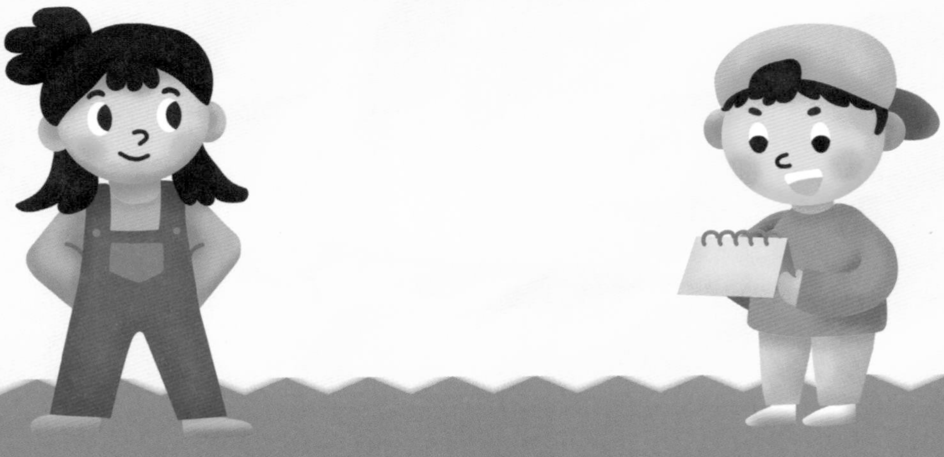

★ [1 ~ 60] 다음 사진과 우리말을 보고 영작하시오.

1

기차가 멈췄다.

12쪽

2

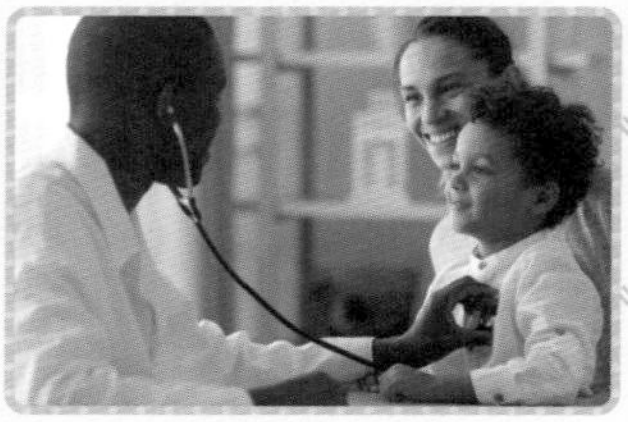

나는 병원에서 일한다.

15쪽

3

Steve는 아침 9시에 일어났다.

15쪽

4

내 어머니는 예술가이다.

18쪽

5

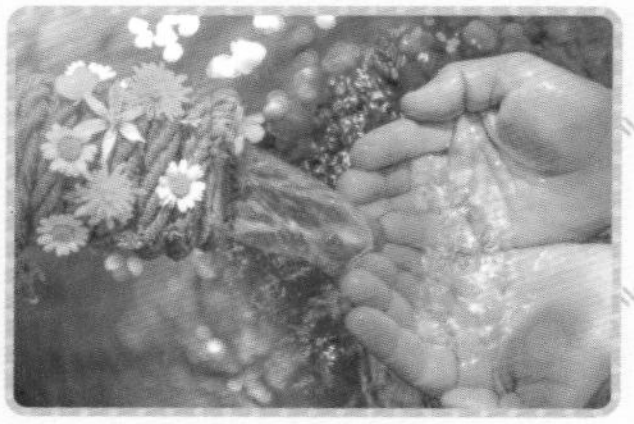

물은 아주 중요하다.

21쪽

6

내가 가장 좋아하는 과목은 영어이다.

21쪽

7

나는 10장의 우표를 필요로 한다.

24쪽

8

Nora는 그녀의 가방들을 꾸미기 시작했다.

27쪽

9

우리는 휴대폰들로 많은 유용한 것들을 한다.

27쪽

10

나는 그에게 약간의 돈을 주었다.

30쪽

11

Jason은 나에게 그 레고 성을 주었다.

33쪽

12

내 부모님께서 나에게 그들의 옛 사진들을 보여주셨다.

33쪽

13

소금은 우리의 음식을 맛있게 만든다.

36쪽

14

그 결말은 모든 사람들을 울게 만들었다.

39쪽

15

나의 바보같은 실수들이 그들을 화나게 만들었다.

39쪽

16

나는 내 여가시간에 테니스 치는 것을 즐긴다.

44쪽

17

그녀는 아름다운 눈을 가지고 있다.

47쪽

18

우리들은 휴대폰들로 영화들을 만든다.

47쪽

19

나는 내 숙제를 끝마쳤다.

51쪽

20

나는 어제 내 다리가 부러졌다.

53쪽

21

나는 언젠가 너를 위해 그것을 연주할 것이다.

53쪽

22

그는 벤치에서 책을 읽는 중이다.

56쪽

23

그들은 학교에서 이리저리 걷고 있는 중이었다.

59쪽

24

나는 홍콩에 관한 TV 프로그램을 시청하는 중이었다.

59쪽

25

나는 Sam을 10년 동안 알아왔다.

62쪽

26

“Good luck” 동전들은 자연의 경이로운 경관들을 망가뜨려왔다.

65쪽

27

그들은 오랫동안 나에게 잘 대해줬다.

65쪽

28

우리는 막 그 프로젝트를 끝냈다.

68쪽

29

나는 전에 그 가수를 본 적이 있다.

71쪽

30

우리는 이미 점심 식사를 했다.

71쪽

31

우리는 휴대폰으로 많은 유용한 것을 할 수 있다.

76쪽

32

제가 신용카드로 지불할 수 있을까요?

79쪽

33

관광은 자연 지역들에 손상을 줄 수 있다.

79쪽

34

이것은 쉽지 않을 지도 모른다.

82쪽

35

그 광고는 재밌어 보일지도 모른다.

85쪽

36

응급실 의사는 특별한 옷을 입을지도 모른다.

85쪽

37

우리는 그들을 돌봐야 한다.

88쪽

38

그것은 재미있을 것이 틀림없다.

91쪽

39

너는 여기서 자전거를 타지 말아야 한다.

91쪽

40

사람들은 금으로 지불하곤 했다.

94쪽

41

사람들은 칼로 싸우곤 했다.

97쪽

42

나는 서커스에서 광대들을 좋아하곤 했다.

97쪽

43

나는 더 일찍 도착했어야 하는데.

100쪽

44

그는 저 모든 소음 속에서 잠을 잤을 리가 없다.

103쪽

45

그 알약들은 그를 도와줬을 런지도 모른다.

103쪽

46

금이 그 광산에서 발견된다.

108쪽

47

많은 사진들이 내 삼촌에 의해 촬영된다.

111쪽

48

그 나무집은 두 명의 건축업자들에 의해 지어진다.

111쪽

49 

그것은 약 500년 전에 지어졌다.

114쪽

50 

물이 가스렌지 위에서 끓여지고 있는 중이다.

117쪽

51 

그 케이크는 오븐에서 구워졌다.

117쪽

52 

새 경기장이 여기에 지어질 것이다.

120쪽

53 

Monopoly는 전 세계에서 플레이 되어져 왔다.

123쪽

54 

모든 그릇들은 식사 후에 반드시 세척되어야 한다.

123쪽

55 

그들은 보드 게임에 관심이 있다.

126쪽

56 

그들은 그 새 집에 만족했다.

129쪽

57 

그 산의 꼭대기는 눈으로 덮여 있었다.

129쪽

58 

사자는 그것의 발톱에 의해 알 수 있다.

132쪽

59 

David은 아주 빠른 운전자로 알려져 있었다.

135쪽

60 

그것은 그것의 수공예 제품들로 알려져 있다.

135쪽

Answers
정답

DAY 01 주어 + 동사

개념확인문제 001 (본문13쪽)

1 ① 2 ① 3 ②

개념확인문제 002 (본문 13쪽)

The truck behind you came on time.

혼공연습 (본문 14쪽)

A ① He ran to the bus stop.
S V
② Spring begins in March.
S V
③ She went to the library after school.
S V

B ① go to school at eight
② live with my parents
③ go to a Chinese class every Saturday

C ① lives, (K)orea
② lives, (B)razil
③ lives in, (C)hina

혼공완성 (본문 15쪽)

A ① I work in a hospital.
② Steve woke up at nine in the morning.

B ① A new student moved to my class.
② I go to bed at eight at night.
③ I played with them in the evening.

C ① 제주도 ② 비행기 ③ 5 ④ 한라산

혼공복습 (본문 16쪽)

A ① He, stopped
② went, to
③ works, day
④ truck, time

B ① He ran to the bus stop.
② Spring begins in March.
③ She went to the library after school.
④ I live with my parents.

C ① I work in a hospital.
② Steve woke up at nine in the morning.
③ A new student moved to my class.
④ I go to bed at eight at night.
⑤ I played with them in the evening.

D ① 내 가족과 나는 지난 여름에 제주도에 갔다.
② 우리는 비행기로 거기에 갔다.
③ 우리는 5일 동안 거기에 머물렀다.
④ 우리는 한라산 꼭대기까지 등산을 했다.

DAY 02 주어 + 동사 + 보어

개념확인문제 001 (본문 19쪽)

1 ② 2 ① 3 ①

개념확인문제 002 (본문 19쪽)

I often feel sleepy and tired.

혼공연습 (본문 20쪽)

A ① Yesterday was Parents' Day.
S V C
② Your computer looks nice.
S V C
③ I am good at Korean.
S V C

B ① am not an animal
② is a morning person
③ is so nice

C ① 숲은 / 매우 중요하다 / 우리에게
② 스포츠는 / 좋다 / 너의 건강과 정신에

혼공완성 (본문 21쪽)

A ① Water is very important.
② My favorite subject is English.

B ① Coco is my pet dog.
② Yesterday was my sister's wedding day.
③ Climbing on rainy days is dangerous.
Climbing is dangerous on rainy days.

C 잘못된 문장
① 클로이는 항상 한가해 보인다
② 그녀는 건강하고 활동적이지 않다

바른 해석
① 클로이는 항상 바빠 보인다
② 그녀는 건강하고 활동적이다

혼공복습 (본문 22쪽)

A ① car, looks
② soup, tastes
③ idea, sounds
④ often, tired

B ① Yesterday was Parents' Day.
② I am good at Korean.
③ I am not an animal.
④ She is a morning person.

C ① Water is very important.
② My favorite subject is English.
English is my favorite subject.
③ Coco is my pet dog.
My pet dog is Coco.
④ Yesterday was my sister's wedding day.
My sister's wedding day was yesterday.
⑤ Climbing on rainy days is dangerous.
Climbing is dangerous on rainy days.

D ① 클로이는 항상 바빠 보인다.
② 그녀는 저녁형 인간이 아니다.
③ 그녀가 가장 좋아하는 스포츠는 수영과 테니스이다.
④ 그녀는 건강하고 활동적이다.

DAY 03 주어 + 동사 + 목적어

개념확인문제 001 (본문 25쪽)

1 ② 2 ① 3 ②

개념확인문제 002 (본문 25쪽)

My mom made *bibimbap* for us.

혼공연습 (본문 26쪽)

A ① He left his bag at home.
S V O
② She saved money for them.
S V O
③ I lost my movie ticket on the subway.
S V O

B ① saw many stars in the sky
② gave a concert at the park
③ watered some plants

C ① 나는 / 보통 / 나의 숙제를 시작한다 / 밤 늦게
② 나의 강아지는 / 큰 귀를 가지고 있다 / 그리고 짧은 다리를

혼공완성 (본문 27쪽)

A ① Nora started packing her bags.
② We do many useful things with cell phones.

B ① Many people like climbing mountains.
② The builders used many amazing building techniques.
③ He never missed practice for any reason.

C 번호: ③
해석: 물은 매우 중요하다.

혼공복습 (본문 28쪽)

A ① faced, strong
② cleaned, room
③ Korea, seasons
④ made, us

B ① He left his bag at home.
② She saved money for them.
③ I lost my movie ticket on the subway.
④ We saw many stars in the sky.

C ① I usually start my homework late at night.
② Nora started packing her bags.
③ We do many useful things with cell phones.
④ People like climbing many mountains.
Many people like climbing mountains.
⑤ He never missed practice for any reason.

D ① 너는 너의 시야를 넓힐 수 있다.
② 그는 매우 심하게 그의 등을 다쳤다.
③ 물은 매우 중요하다.
④ 수컷은 블루베리들의 즙으로 둥지를 칠한다.

DAY 04 주어 + 동사 + 목1 + 목2

개념확인문제 001 (본문 31쪽)

1 ① 2 ② 3 ②

개념확인문제 002 (본문 31쪽)

My uncle bought a new computer for me.

혼공연습 본문 32쪽

A ① It gives you some exercise.
S V O1 O2

② Ms. Kim teaches us Spanish.
S V O1 O2

③ My mom always makes me delicious food.
S V O1 O2

B ① sent me the schedule
② showed me a video
③ lent us her phone

C ① 숲은 / 준다 / 우리들에게 / 신선한 공기를
② 내 아버지는 / 항상 / 보낸다 / 나에게 / 문자를 / 방과 후에

혼공완성 본문 33쪽

A ① Jason gave me the Lego castle.
② My parents showed me their old pictures.

B ① The pirates gave her the secret ring.
② Malfoy told him where to go.
③ The police officer asked me a lot of questions about the guy.

C ① to us
② of the movie director

혼공복습 본문 34쪽

A ① gave, job
② told, everything
③ bought, computer
④ asked, questions

B ① Ms. Kim teaches us Spanish.
② My mom always makes me delicious food.
③ Forests give us fresh air.
④ My father always sends me text messages after school.

C ① Jason gave me the Lego castle.
② My parents showed me their old pictures.
③ The pirates gave her the secret ring.
④ Malfoy told him where to go.
⑤ The police officer asked me a lot of questions about the guy.

D ① to us
② of the movie director
③ for me

DAY 05 주어 + 동사 + 목적어 + 목적보어

개념확인문제 001 본문 37쪽

1 ② 2 ① 3 ①

개념확인문제 002 본문 37쪽

He also makes us laugh a lot.

혼공연습 본문 38쪽

A ① It makes your mind calm.
S V O O.C.

② Dr. Park advised me to work out regularly.
S V O O.C.

③ Riding bicycles instead of driving cars
S

can keep it clean.
V O O.C.

B ① keep rivers clean
② asks him to help
③ wants us to fight back

C ① 더러운 물은 / 만든다 / 식물들과 동물들을 / 아프게
② 스포츠를 하는 것은 / 만들 수 있다 / 너의 몸을 / 강하게

혼공완성 본문 39쪽

A ① The ending made everyone cry.
② My silly mistakes made them angry.

B ① He was watching Mrs. Harris raise the school flag.
② People elected Lincoln their president.
③ He wanted me to listen to the song.

C hard, work, helped, win, competition

혼공복습 본문 40쪽

A ① named, dog
② found, empty
③ heard, shout
④ makes, laugh

B ① It makes your mind calm.
② Riding bicycles instead of driving cars can keep it clean.
③ Hogwarts wants us to fight back.
④ Dirty water makes plants and animals sick.

C ① Playing sports can make your body strong.
② The ending made everyone cry.
③ My silly mistakes made them angry.
④ People elected Lincoln their president.
⑤ He wanted me to listen to the song.

D ① 소금은 우리의 음식을 맛있게 만든다.
② 그녀는 그녀의 이웃이 거기에 서 있는 것을 보았다.
③ 나의 부모님은 내가 과학자가 되기를 원하신다.
④ 스텔라의 노력은 결국 그녀가 전국 수영 대회에서 우승하도록 도와주었다.

DAY 06 현재

개념확인문제 001 (본문 45쪽)

1 ① 2 ① 3 ②

개념확인문제 002 (본문 45쪽)

The sun sets in the west.

혼공연습 (본문 46쪽)

A ① 가까운 미래
② 반복되는 일
③ 현재상황

B ① like listening to music
② like our school food
③ play baseball with the team after school

C ① 스포츠는 중요하다 / 우리의 건강에
② 우체국은 닫는다 / 5시 30분에

혼공완성 (본문 47쪽)

A ① She has beautiful eyes.
② We make movies with cell phones.

B ① Tourism brings money into a country.
② Breakfast gives you energy for the day.
③ Rivers have many benefits.

C 나이: (14)살 좋아하는 운동: (축구)
숙제하는 시간: (늦은) 밤
어려워하는 점: (사람들 앞에서 말하는 것)

혼공복습 (본문 48쪽)

A ① enjoy, free
② looks, rabbit
③ museum, opens
④ medicine, bitter

B ① The sun sets in the west.
② My friends always copy my homework.
③ I play baseball with the team after school.
④ Sports are important for your health.

C ① She has beautiful eyes.
② We make movies with cell phones.
③ Tourism brings money into a country.
④ Breakfast gives you energy for the day.
⑤ Rivers have many benefits.

D ① 나는 14살이다.
② 나는 운동장에서 축구를 하는 것을 좋아한다.
③ 나는 보통 밤 늦게 숙제를 시작한다.
④ 나는 사람들 앞에서 말하는 것에 어려움이 있다.

DAY 07 과거 / 미래

개념확인문제 001 (본문 51쪽)

1 ② 2 ② 3 ②

개념확인문제 002 (본문 51쪽)

I am going to tell you about my mom.

혼공연습 (본문 52쪽)

A ① became
② will stay
③ will spend

B ① lost my movie ticket on the subway
② am going to travel there by bus
③ started writing computer programs at the age of thirteen

C ① 내 컴퓨터는 / 지난 밤에 작동하지 않았다
② 우리는 / 또한 비디오를 제작할 것이다

혼공완성 (본문 53쪽)

A ① I broke my leg yesterday.
② I will play it for you someday.

B ① He put on his clothes.
② I didn't bring my umbrella.
③ John read a book about Korean history.

C 잘못된 단어: (C) 바른 단어: are

혼공복습 (본문 54쪽)

A ① finished, homework
② won, contest
③ will, front
④ going, tell

B ① Dr. Smith became a doctor in 1930.
② They will spend all day swimming at the beach.
③ I am going to travel there by bus.
④ He started writing computer programs at the age of thirteen.

C ① My computer didn't work last night.
② I broke my leg yesterday.
③ He put on his clothes.
④ I didn't bring my umbrella.
⑤ John read a book about Korean history.

D ① 나는 이번 여름에 내 가족들과 전주에 갔다.
② 우리는 거기에 KTX를 타고 갔다.
③ 우리는 한옥 마을을 방문했고 거기서 비빔밥을 먹었다.
④ 우리는 내년 여름에 전주를 방문할 예정이다.

DAY 08 진행형

개념확인문제 001 (본문 57쪽)

1 ① 2 ② 3 ②

개념확인문제 002 (본문 57쪽)

They will be waiting for you at the airport.

혼공연습 (본문 58쪽)

A ① is wearing
② was moving
③ will be playing

B ① was washing a car in the driveway
② are being so nice
③ were not crossing the road

C ① 우리는 / 계획하고 있는 중이다 / 마을 홈페이지를 만들려고
② 지구는 / 죽어가고 있다 / 쓰레기 때문에

혼공완성 (본문 59쪽)

A ① They were walking around at school.
② I was watching a TV program on Hong Kong.

B ① David is running for class president.
② They are having a bad day.
③ She was expressing her disappointment.

C (A) are sinking
(B) are disappearing

혼공복습 (본문 60쪽)

A ① reading, bench
② talking, phone
③ was, arriving
④ will, waiting

B ① My sister is wearing a white dress.
② He will be playing the drums in the choir room.
③ The kids were not crossing the road.
④ We are planning to create a town homepage.

C ① The earth is dying because of trash.
② I was watching a TV program on Hong Kong.
③ David is running for class president.
④ They are having a bad day.
⑤ She was expressing her disappointment.

D ① 제니는 그녀의 개와 공원을 걷고 있는 중이다.
② 그는 책상을 옮기는 중이다.
③ 섬들이 바다로 가라앉고 있는 중이다.
④ 재규어는 야생에서 사라지고 있는 중이다.

DAY 09 현재완료 1

개념확인문제 001 (본문 63쪽)

1 ② 2 ① 3 ①

개념확인문제 002 (본문 63쪽)

How long have you taught math?

혼공연습 (본문 64쪽)

A ① has written
② have known
③ has kept

B ① has lived in New York for two months
② has waited for her little sister for three hours
③ have gathered information for a long time

C ① 그 때 이후로 / 에릭은 / 다른 매우 높은 산들을 등반해 왔다
② 거의 1년이 되었다 / 내 학생들과 내가 너의 학교를 방문한 이후로

혼공완성 본문 65쪽

A ① "Good luck" coins have ruined natural wonders.
② They have been good to me for a long time.

B ① My dad has exercised regularly for three months.
② There have been serious arguments between them.
③ He has never lived in Busan.

C have succeeded

혼공복습 본문 66쪽

A ① known, years
② has, since
③ have, lived
④ long, taught

B ① My mom has kept the back door open all day.
② Tom has lived in New York for two months.
③ She has waited for her little sister for three hours.
④ We have gathered information for a long time.

C ① Erik has climbed other very tall mountains since then.
② "Good luck" coins have ruined natural wonders.
③ They have been good to me for a long time.
④ My dad has exercised regularly for three months.
⑤ There have been serious arguments between them.

D ① 내 학생들과 내가 너의 학교에 방문한지 벌써 거의 일 년이 되었다.
② 그는 절대 부산에서 산 적이 없다.
③ 지금까지 약 5,000명의 사람들이 에베레스트 산 정상에 등반하는데 성공했다.

DAY 10 현재완료 2

개념확인문제 001 본문 69쪽

1 ② 2 ② 3 ①

개념확인문제 002 본문 69쪽

My Spanish teacher has never been to Spain.

혼공연습 본문 70쪽

A ① yet
② ever
③ already

B ① have never been to a foreign country
② has been to Jeju-do twice
③ has just released a new album

C ① 우리는 / 제임스를 만난 적이 있다 / 세 번
② 나는 / 내 일기장을 잃어버렸다

혼공완성 본문 71쪽

A ① I have seen the singer before.
② We have already had lunch.

B ① I have already arrived here.
② We have never tried Indian food before.
③ Have you ever seen this movie?

C (1) Jihoo, three
(2) Sumin, three, times

혼공복습 본문 72쪽

A ① just, finished
② have, already
③ has, before
④ never, been

B ① Your effort hasn't paid off yet.
② They have already gone to bed.
③ I have never been to a foreign country.
④ She has been to Jeju-do twice.

C ① BTS has just released a new album.
② We have met James three times.
③ I have seen the singer before.
④ We have already had lunch.
⑤ I have already arrived here.

D ① 우리는 절대 이전에 인도 음식을 먹어본 적이 없다.
② 너는 이 영화를 본 적이 있니?
③ 지후는 제주도에 세 번 가본 적이 있다.
④ 수민이는 경주에 두 번 가본 적이 있다.

DAY 11 조동사 can / could

개념확인문제 001 본문 77쪽

1 ① 2 ① 3 ②

개념확인문제 002 본문 77쪽

I couldn't finish my homework.

혼공연습 본문 78쪽

A ① can understand
② can have
③ can be

B ① can carry these boxes for the old lady
② could not find a job
③ can be a big help to your project

C ① 때때로 / 등반하는 것은 / 위험할 수 있다
② 너는 / 새 컴퓨터들을 사용해도 된다 / 언제라도 / 학교에 있는 시간 동안

혼공완성 본문 79쪽

A ① Could I pay by credit card?
② Tourism can damage natural areas.

B ① We can make clothes with *hanji*.
② Cell phones can cause problems in public places.
③ She could not get on the ride because of her height.

C can't, take, can't, drink

혼공복습 본문 80쪽

A ① can, useful
② able, message
③ could, rain
④ finish, homework

B ① You can have fun playing in the mud.
② You can be healthy and happy.
③ I can be a big help to your project.
④ Sometimes climbing can be dangerous. Climbing can be sometimes dangerous.

C ① Could I pay by credit card?
② Tourism can damage natural areas.
③ We can make clothes with *hanji*.
④ Cell phones can cause problems in public places.
⑤ She could not get on the ride because of her height.

D ① 당신은 이 미술관에서 사진을 찍을 수 없어요.
② 오, 알겠어요.
③ 그러면, 제가 이 버거를 여기서 먹을 수 있을까요?
④ 아니요, 당신은 안에서 어떤 것도 먹거나 마실 수 없어요.

DAY 12 조동사 may / might

개념확인문제 001 본문 83쪽

1 ② 2 ① 3 ①

개념확인문제 002 본문 83쪽

This expectation might be wrong.

혼공연습 본문 84쪽

A ① may go
② may be
③ may call

B ① may go there at any moment
② might not be children
③ might see that new action movie

C ① 너는 / 착용하는 것을 좋아하지 않을 것 같다 / 자전거 헬멧을
② 너는 / 하이킹하러 가는 것을 원하지 않을 것 같다 / 너의 부모님과

혼공완성 본문 85쪽

A ① The ad may look fun.
② An emergency room doctor may wear special clothes.

B ① Mr. Kim might feel bad because of the rumors.
② You may repeat the behavior many times.

③ A doctor's white coat may have a negative effect.

C young, America, may(might), see, year

혼공복습 본문 86쪽

A ① not, easy
② habits, harm
③ Losing, feel
④ expectation, wrong

B ① It may be true.
② He may call me back.
③ You may go there at any moment.
④ He might see that new action movie.

C ① You may not like to wear a bike helmet.
② You may not want to go hiking with your parents.
③ An emergency room doctor may wear special clothes.
④ Mr. Kim might feel bad because of the rumors.
⑤ You may repeat the behavior many times.

D ① 제가 주문을 받아도 될까요?
② 그 광고는 재밌게 보일지도 모른다.
③ 의사의 흰색 코트는 부정적인 영향을 미칠지도 모른다.
④ 북미의 젊은 사람은 매년 4만 개의 TV 광고를 볼지도 모른다.

DAY 13 조동사 should / must

개념확인문제 001 본문 89쪽

1 ① 2 ② 3 ②

개념확인문제 002 본문 89쪽

He must be thirsty after running.

혼공연습 본문 90쪽

A ① have to do
② has to wear
③ has to be

B ① must not eat food in the room
② should be polite to others
③ have to clean your room

C ① 우리들은 / 반드시 아침식사를 맨 먼저 해야한다
② 그는 / 좋은 선생님인 것이 틀림없다

혼공완성 본문 91쪽

A ① It must be enjoyable.
② You shouldn't ride a bike here.

B ① She must be a superhero.
② You must go to bed early tonight.
③ We should follow the rules of the museum.

C (1) 집에 도착하고 난 후
(2) 기침하고 난 후
(3) 음식을 먹기 전에

혼공복습 본문 92쪽

A ① take, them
② be, final
③ have, on
④ must, thirsty

B ① She must be home by ten o'clock.
② You must not eat food in the room.
③ You should be polite to others.
④ You have to clean your room.

C ① It must be enjoyable.
② You shouldn't ride a bike here.
③ She must be a superhero.
④ You must go to bed early tonight.
⑤ We should follow the rules of the museum.

D ① 그는 좋은 선생님인 것이 틀림없다.
② 너는 집에 도착한 후에 너의 손을 씻어야 한다.
③ 너는 기침을 한 후에 너의 손을 씻어야 한다.
④ 너는 음식을 먹기 전에 너의 손을 씻어야 한다.

DAY 14 기타 조동사

개념확인문제 001 본문 95쪽

1 ① 2 ① 3 ②

개념확인문제 002 본문 95쪽

You had better not use your smartphone during class.

혼공연습 본문 96쪽

A ① 과거의 습관
② 과거의 상태
③ 과거의 습관

B ① used to be a park
② used to be very weak
③ would visit his grandparents on weekends

C ① 내 아버지는 / 우리들에게 들려주시곤 했다 / 잠잘 때 이야기들을
② 너는 / 먹는 것이 낫다 / 더 많은 과일과 채소를

혼공완성 본문 97쪽

A ① People would fight with swords.
② I used to like the clowns at the circus.

B ① The town used to be very crowded.
② You had better put on your coat.
③ Mrs. Brown used to live next door.

C ① 런던
② 쵸콜렛
③ 금발
④ 걸어(서)

혼공복습 본문 98쪽

A ① used, pay
② go, school
③ There, be
④ better, use

B ① I used to keep a diary.
② There used to be a post office here.
③ The hotel used to be a park.
④ Bill would visit his grandparents on weekends.

C ① People would fight with swords.
② I used to like the clowns at the circus.
③ The town used to be very crowded.
④ You had better put on your coat.
⑤ Mrs. Brown used to live next door.

D ① 나는 예전에 런던에 살았었다.
② 나는 쵸콜렛을 좋아했었다.
③ 나는 머리색이 금발이었다.
④ 나는 매일 학교에 걸어서 다녔었다.

DAY 15 조동사 + have + p.p.

개념확인문제 001 본문 101쪽

1 ① 2 ② 3 ②

개념확인문제 002 본문 101쪽

She should have finished it by the middle of the week.

혼공연습 본문 102쪽

A ① may have left
② must have entered
③ could have won

B ① must have fallen from the roof
② might have stopped
③ can't have been his car

C ① 그 사고는 / 더 심할 수도 있었다
② 너는 / 왔어야 하는데 / 학교 축제에

혼공완성 본문 103쪽

A ① He can't have slept through all that noise.
② The pills might have helped him.

B ① They could have missed the train.
② The scientist may have solved the riddle of Saturn's rings.
③ He must have disturbed your birthday party.

C gate, broken, seen, coffee

혼공복습 본문 104쪽

A ① should, arrived
② been, hurt
③ should, door
④ finished, middle

B ① Someone must have entered my room.
② We could have won without you.
③ He must have fallen from the roof.
④ The rain might have stopped.

C ① The accident could have been worse.
② He can't have slept through all that noise.
③ The pills might have helped him.
④ They could have missed the train.
⑤ The scientist may have solved the riddle of Saturn's rings.

Ⓓ ① 누군가 실수로 문을 열어두고 간 게 틀림없다.
② 누군가 접시를 깬 것이 틀림없다.
③ 누군가 도둑을 보았을 지도 모른다.
④ 누군가 탁자에 약간의 커피를 쏟았을 수도 있다.

DAY 16 능동태 / 수동태

개념확인문제 001 (본문 109쪽)

1 ② 2 ① 3 ①

개념확인문제 002 (본문 109쪽)

Fresh milk is delivered from the farm every morning.

혼공연습 (본문 110쪽)

Ⓐ ① is visited
② is cooked
③ are caused

Ⓑ ① is used all over the world
② are never mentioned again
are mentioned never again
③ are fired by company every year

Ⓒ ① 숲은 / 파괴된다 / 인간에 의해
② 그 이야기는 / 쓰여지지 않는다 / 프랑스어로

혼공완성 (본문 111쪽)

Ⓐ ① A lot of photos are taken by my uncle.
② The treehouse is built by two famous builders.

Ⓑ ① The jazz festival is held in June.
② Popular actors are invited by the government.
③ The main character is played by Scarlett Johansson.

Ⓒ located, visited

혼공복습 (본문 112쪽)

Ⓐ ① found, mine
② sing, song
③ read, languages
④ delivered, farm

Ⓑ ① English is used all over the world.
② Many workers are fired by the company every year.
③ The forests are destroyed by humans.
④ The story is not written in French.

Ⓒ ① A lot of photos are taken by my uncle.
② The treehouse is built by two famous builders.
③ The jazz festival is held in June.
④ Popular actors are invited by the government.
⑤ The main character is played by Scarlett Johansson.

Ⓓ ① 모든 식사는 신선한 음식으로 요리된다.
② 큰 문제들은 내 남동생에 의해서 유발된다.
③ 앙코르 와트는 캄보디아 북서쪽에 위치 해있다.
④ 앙코르 와트는 해마다 많은 관광객에 의해서 방문된다.

DAY 17 수동태의 시제 1

개념확인문제 001 (본문 115쪽)

1 ② 2 ① 3 ②

개념확인문제 002 (본문 115쪽)

These trees are being grown for timber.

혼공연습 (본문 116쪽)

Ⓐ ① was prepared
② was cleaned
③ was put out

Ⓑ ① were given a toy at PIZZA LOCA
② were watered by my mother
③ were taken by the students

Ⓒ ① 표들은 / 팔리고 있는 중이었다 / 300달러에
② 너무 많은 쓰레기들이 / 버려지고 있는 중이다 / 바다에

혼공완성 (본문 117쪽)

Ⓐ ① Water is being boiled on the stove.
② The cake was baked in the oven.

Ⓑ ① A beauty salon is being run in our area.
② The Eiffel Tower was completed in 1889.
③ Two women were being interviewed by the police.

C (1) was written
(2) were built
(3) was invented
(4) was served

혼공복습 (본문 118쪽)

A ① was, built
② named, uncle
③ being, punished
④ trees, grown

B ① A hotel room was prepared for them.
② The fire was put out by the fire fighters.
③ The tests were taken by the students.
④ Tickets were being sold for $300.

C ① Too much waste is being dumped at sea.
② Water is being boiled on the stove.
③ The cake was baked in the oven.
④ A beauty salon is being run in our area.
⑤ Two women were being interviewed by the police.

D ① 해리포터 시리즈는 J.K.롤링에 의해서 쓰여졌다.
② 피라미드는 파라오들을 위해 지어졌다.
③ 전구는 토마스 에디슨에 의해서 발명되었다.
④ 첫 번째 맥도날드 햄버거는 1955년에 제공되었다.

DAY 18 수동태의 시제 2

개념확인문제 001 (본문 121쪽)

1 ② 2 ① 3 ②

개념확인문제 002 (본문 121쪽)

The office has already been cleaned.

혼공연습 (본문 122쪽)

A ① can be eaten
② must be produced
③ may(might) be directed/ could be directed

B ① has been cooked by my father on Sundays
② will be enjoyed in more countries/
will be enjoyed more in countries
③ have been painted by the students

C ① 그 식물들은 / 물이 뿌려져 왔다 / 지난 달 이후로
② 새로운 요리책이 / 발간될 것이다 / 내년에

혼공완성 (본문 123쪽)

A ① Monopoly has been played all over the world.
② All the dishes must be washed after the meal.

B ① All drinks may be included in the price.
② The national park has been visited by many tourists.
③ The match must have been finished.

C (1) washed
(2) read
(3) done
(4) cleaned

혼공복습 (본문 124쪽)

A ① will, built
② will, made
③ can, emptied
④ has, cleaned

B ① The movie may be directed by Christopher Nolan.
② Lunch has been cooked by my father on Sundays.
③ The plants have been watered since last month.
④ A new cookbook will be released next year.

C ① Monopoly has been played all over the world.
② All the dishes must be washed after the meal.
③ All drinks may be included in the price.
④ The national park has been visited by many tourists.
⑤ The match must have been finished.

D ① 더러운 옷들은 집에서 세탁되어져야 한다.
② 적어도 하루에 한 권의 책이 읽혀져야 한다.
③ 숙제는 아침에 완료되어야 한다.
④ 지미의 방은 매일 청소되어져야 한다.

DAY 19 수동태의 관용표현 1

개념확인문제 001 (본문 127쪽)

1 ① 2 ② 3 ①

개념확인문제 002 (본문 127쪽)

Paul's face was filled with anger.

혼공연습 (본문 128쪽)

A ① filled
② caught
③ disappointed

B ① was filled with people
② was covered with frost
③ was disappointed by her attitude

C ① 그는 / 관심이 없었다 / 꽃을 키우는 것에 / 정원에서
② 건물의 앞면이 / 덮여 있었다 / 담쟁이로

혼공완성 (본문 129쪽)

A ① They were satisfied with the new house.
② The top of the mountain was covered with snow.

B ① We are not satisfied with these results.
② The dawn was filled with the sound of birds.
③ Sophie's notebook is covered with stickers.

C ① with
② in
③ with
④ with

혼공복습 (본문 130쪽)

A ① interested, in
② satisfied, with
③ engaged, business
④ filled, with

B ① The park was filled with people.
② The grass was covered with frost.
③ I was disappointed by her attitude.
④ He wasn't interested in growing flowers in the garden.

C ① They were satisfied with the new house.
② The top of the mountain was covered with snow.
③ We are not satisfied with these results.
④ The dawn was filled with the sound of birds.
⑤ Sophie's notebook is covered with stickers.

D ① 나는 그의 대답이 만족스럽지 않다.
② 그는 요가에 깊은 관심이 있었다.
③ 그의 얼굴은 주름으로 덮여 있었다.
④ 공기는 꽃들의 향기로 가득차 있었다.

DAY 20 수동태의 관용표현 2

개념확인문제 001 (본문 133쪽)

1 ① 2 ① 3 ②

개념확인문제 002 (본문 133쪽)

Drinking is known to be bad for your health.

혼공연습 (본문 134쪽)

A ① by
② to
③ as

B ① was known for her kindness to all
was known to all for her kindness
② is known to the police
③ is known for his good looks

C ① 사람은 / 알 수 있다 / 친구로 / 그가 사귀는
② 흡연은 / 알려져 있다 / 한 사람의 위험을 높이는 것으로 / 폐암을 생기게 하는

혼공완성 (본문 135쪽)

A ① David was known as a very fast driver.
② It is known for its handicraft products.

B ① This area is known as Soho of New York.
② A bird may be known by its songs.
③ The French are known as a food-loving people.

C ① Bong Joon-ho is known for his movie, *Parasite*.
② The Curies are best known for discovering radium.
③ South Africa is well known for its diamond mines.
④ Sodium chloride is known as salt.

혼공복습

(본문 136쪽)

A ① known, by
② was, as
③ known, sense
④ known, health

B ① She was known for her kindness to all.
She was known to all for her kindness.
② This man is known to the police.
③ He is known for his good looks.
④ Smoking is known to increase a person's risk of developing lung cancer.

C ① David was known as a very fast driver.
② It is known for its handicraft products.
③ This area is known as Soho of New York.
④ A bird may be known by its songs.
⑤ The French are known as a food-loving people.

D ① 봉준호는 그의 영화 '기생충'으로 유명하다.
② 퀴리부부는 라듐을 발견한 것으로 가장 잘 알려져 있다.
③ 남아프리카는 그곳의 다이아몬드 광산으로 잘 알려져 있다.
④ 염화나트륨은 소금으로 알려져 있다.

★ Special 60 문장 ★

본문 140쪽

1 The train stopped.
2 I work in a hospital.
3 Steve woke up at nine in the morning.
4 My mother is an artist.
5 Water is very important.
6 My favorite subject is English.
7 I need 10 stamps.
8 Nora started packing her bags.
9 We do many useful things with cell phones.
10 I gave him some money.
11 Jason gave me the Lego castle.
12 My parents showed me their old pictures.
13 Salt makes our food tasty.
14 The ending made everyone cry.
15 My silly mistakes made them angry.
16 I enjoy playing tennis in my free time.
17 She has beautiful eyes.
18 We make movies with cell phones.
19 I finished my homework.
20 I broke my leg yesterday.
21 I will play it for you someday.
22 He is reading a book on the bench.
23 They were walking around at school.
24 I was watching a TV program on Hong Kong.
25 I have known Sam for 10 years.
26 "Good luck" coins have ruined natural wonders.
27 They have been good to me for a long time.
28 We have just finished the project.
29 I have seen the singer before.
30 We have already had lunch.
31 We can do many useful things with cell phones.
32 Could I pay by credit card?
33 Tourism can damage natural areas.
34 This may not be easy.
35 The ad may look fun.
36 An emergency room doctor may wear special clothes.
37 We should take care of them.
38 It must be enjoyable.
39 You shouldn't ride a bike here.
40 People used to pay in gold.
41 People would fight with swords.
42 I used to like the clowns at the circus.
43 I should have arrived earlier.
44 He can't have slept through all that noise.
45 The pills might have helped him.
46 Gold is found in the mine.
47 A lot of photos are taken by my uncle.
48 The treehouse is built by two famous builders.
49 It was built about 500 years ago.
50 Water is being boiled on the stove.
51 The cake was baked in the oven.
52 A new stadium will be built here.
53 Monopoly has been played all over the world.
54 All the dishes must be washed after the meal.
55 They are interested in board games.
56 They were satisfied with the new house.
57 The top of the mountain was covered with snow.
58 The lion is known by its claws.
59 David was known as a very fast driver.
60 It is known for its handicraft products.

★ Memo ★

★ Memo ★

★ Memo ★

★ Memo ★